Florence Nonotuck silk company

Florence home needle-work 1896

Florence Nonotuck silk company

Florence home needle-work 1896

ISBN/EAN: 9783741136863

Manufactured in Europe, USA, Canada, Australia, Japa

Cover: Foto ©Lupo / pixelio.de

Manufactured and distributed by brebook publishing software (www.brebook.com)

Florence Nonotuck silk company

Florence home needle-work 1896

COPYRIGHT—1896.

A copy of this book (1896 edition) will be mailed to any address on receipt of three two-cent stamps. In ordering, the year of publication should be mentioned.

There are ten DIFFERENT editions, 1887, 1888, 1889, 1890, 1891, 1892, 1393, 1394, 1395 and 1896, each wholly unlike the others.

One of these will be mailed for six cents, or all for sixty cents.

LATEST EDITION.

FLORENCE, MASS.
NONOTUCK SILK COMPANY.
1896.

CONTENTS.

	PAGE
Centre-pieces and Dollies, Selected Designs,	60
Correct Colors for Embroidery,	71
Corticelli Button-hole Twist,	2d cover
Corticelli Color Card,	82
Corticelli Embroidery Silk,	81, 86
Corticelli Etching Silk,	88
Corticelli Filo Silk,	83, 87
Corticelli Glove-mending Silk,	92
Corticelli Knitting and Crochet Silk,	90
Corticelli Lace Silk,	89
Corticelli Purse Twist,	89
Corticelli Roll Braid,	92
Corticelli Persian Floss,	88
Corticelli Roman Floss,	85
Corticelli Rope Silk,	84, 85
Corticelli Sewing Silk,	2d cover
Corticelli Skirt Protector,	4th cover
Corticelli Whip-cord Crochet Silk,	90
Crocheted Applique Border,	41
Crocheted Silk Bonnet for an Infant,	38
Dollies, Six Prize Patterns,	18
Easter Lily Centre-piece,	15
Embroidered Tea-cloth,	26, 27, 29
Florence Darning Silk,	91
Florence Knitting and Crochet Silk,	91
Florence Natural Silk,	78
Florence Silk Gloves,	78
Florence Silk Mittens,	94, 95
Florence Silk Mosaic,	78
Florence Silk Socks,	93
Florence Silk Underwear,	79
Florence Underwear Silk,	80
Indian Centre-piece,	10
Ivory Soap,	5, 6, 84
Knitted Silk Bonnet for a Child,	31
Knitted Silk Shirt for an Infant,	37
Marking Clothing,	59
Payson's Indelible Ink,	4th cover
Silk Jewels in Embroidery,	45
Sofa Pillow,	22
Stamped Designs, with Price List,	44

INTRODUCTION.

"FLORENCE HOME NEEDLE-WORK"

FOR 1896 is the tenth of a series published annually under this title, the first having been printed in 1887. Like its predecessors, the 1896 edition consists of descriptions of various kinds of work which come properly under this head, and which have been furnished by competent writers on this subject. The descriptions are illustrated by engravings made by our own artists expressly for this edition, and are so clear that we think little difficulty will be experienced by our readers in reproducing the designs in their home needle-work.

The first illustrated chapter is by a writer who has before furnished several articles to this series on various subjects. It will, we hope, receive the same favorable consideration from our readers as have the past contributions. Another contributor furnishes an interesting chapter entitled "Silk Jewels in Embroidery," which has also been well illustrated by our own engraver in a comprehensive manner.

HINTS TO PURCHASERS OF MATERIAL.

In the descriptions of needle-work which are found in the following pages frequent mention is made of suitable material. In the selection of silk threads care is required. Buyers should note carefully the labels on spools and skeins, for the purpose of obtaining a reliable brand, and should note also the size. If a silk thread is to be used on wash material, then it must be a wash silk; hence the importance of the *name*. By reference to the advertising pages the reader will find engravings of spools and skeins of Corticelli Wash Silk. On each skein appears a ticket showing the brand, as well as the size and shade numbers. Light material requires light-weight silk, and coarse, heavy stuff should carry a silk of corresponding size, which is indicated by these labels. Mention has been made by the compiler and contributors of some uses for the various kinds of material and work described under different heads, but we shall expect our readers to discover many other ways to usefully apply the numerous suggestions in needle-work to be found in this collection. We desire to add, however, some information as to silk for knitting, which is of special importance to any one desiring to knit or crochet, as either requires silk of great uniformity in size and quality.

Florence Knitting and Crochet Silk is made of the best quality of *pure* silk the market affords, prepared by combing in a manner similar to that adopted in the preparation of fine wools when intended for knitting purposes. It is *only* in this way that the peculiar "soft finish," so noticeable in all silk threads bearing the *Florence* brand, is obtained. Silk knitting yarns made by combing are *very uniform in size*. They have a *rich, subdued lustre*, which is fully preserved, and even increased, by frequent washings. It is our purpose to offer the *Florence* silk in no shade which will not bear reasonable washing without impairing its beauty of color.

Florence Knitting and Crochet Silk is always sold in one-half-ounce balls. It is made in two sizes, No. 300 (coarse) and No. 500 (fine). In buying, see that the brand FLORENCE is plainly stamped in one end of the wood on which the silk is wound. Both sizes can be obtained in a great variety of colors, matching, each season, all the popular dress and fancy goods shades.

Corticelli Knitting and Crochet Silk is also made of the best quality of *pure* silk, but is *not* prepared by the "combing process," as is the Florence. Instead of this, the fibre is removed from the cocoon by the slower and more expensive method of reeling. This produces a thread of higher

INTRODUCTION.

lustre, which gives it a fine effect. In point of durability there is nothing to be desired in either brand; both are excellent. Those who admire the beautiful gloss of the "Corticelli," and who choose to pay a little more for it, will be pleased by its use; while the many who have in times past admired the soft and "subdued lustre" of the popular and economical "Florence" will continue its use with equal satisfaction and commend it to others. Corticelli Knitting and Crochet Silk is made in many colors in size No. 300 only. Shades of white, however, can be had in size No. 500 also. Both brands are well adapted to crochet or knitting.

CAUTION.

Ladies are cautioned against *all imitations of* FLORENCE and CORTICELLI KNITTING and CROCHET SILK.

Our readers, if using any of the nondescript yarns or so-called knitting silks which we caution them against, although otherwise following the rules laid down in our books, will have no one to blame but themselves if they meet with failure in trying to do good work. To do *good work* one must have the *best silk*. To obtain the *best*, buy only that of established repute. *Brilliancy* and *durability* of *color*, *smoothness* and *evenness* of size in thread, with softness of finish and *freedom* from all deleterious dyestuffs, are the qualities which have established the reputation of these goods. They are for sale by dealers in fine fancy goods everywhere. Ask for them, and do not allow substitutes to be imposed upon you.

WASHING.

In washing articles made from these silks, use a moderate amount of "Ivory" soap, thoroughly dissolved in tepid water. Extract the water by rolling and twisting in a coarse crash towel, after which put in good form and dry *without exposure to the sun*.

Nonotuck Silk Co.,

The Right Way.

Silk Embroidery should never be thrown into the boiler with the common wash; in fact no boiling is needed. All risk of rust or stain is removed by using an earthen wash-bowl in preference to a tin or wooden tub.

Use a pure soap like the "Ivory" which should be chipped and dissolved in warm water to make a suds.

Avoid all doubtful washing compounds, whether solid, fluid, or in the shape of powder.

Wash quickly by squeezing the suds through and through the material, which motion will soon remove all dirt.

Do not use a wash-board, as rubbing may fray the silk. Rinse in clear warm water, and extract the same by placing between two crash towels without exposure to the sun.

Press when very slightly damp with an iron only moderately hot on a soft padded board, the wrong side of the needle-work being uppermost and covered with a clean white cloth.

POPULAR FANCY WORK.

By DOROTHY BRADFORD.

THE interest in needle-work continues unabated in this year of 1896, embroidery, crochet and knitting being leading subjects for the exercise of skill among the lovers of such work. The first of these subjects is perhaps most attractive on account of the great variety of designs now offered.

Schools for instruction in artistic embroidery in many of our cities are graduating good teachers, whose influence is felt among the unprofessional needle-workers in every section. Constant improvement in workmanship is seen, which is due to better teaching, better designs and to the excellence of material.

The most popular foundation for silk embroidery appears to be fine bleached linen, stamped with designs which are executed in washable silk. The favorite articles for the application of this kind of embroidery are centre-pieces, doilies, table covers, photograph frames and sofa pillows, some of which it is the purpose of this article to illustrate and describe. The engravings shown here are from good specimens of needle-work, some of which have received prize medals from recent important expositions. We have not given the same amount of space to crochet and knitting as to embroidery, but the descriptions furnished are interesting and practical for those who love the work.

The selection of colors for silk embroidery is of great importance, and it often perplexes needle-workers who have not ready access to large stocks of material how to make a satisfactory choice. This difficulty is, however, easily overcome by sending twelve cents to the Nonotuck Silk Company, Florence, Mass., who will mail to any address a color card (Fig. 1), showing more than three hundred shades of Corticelli Wash Silk; small samples representing a variety of kinds, differing from each other in size and in twist, are also attached to the card. An experience of nearly sixty years in silk-thread making has given the owners of the brand Corticelli an unequalled reputation, so that purchases of silk bearing this name on spools or tickets can be made with absolute assurance of obtaining the best the market affords.

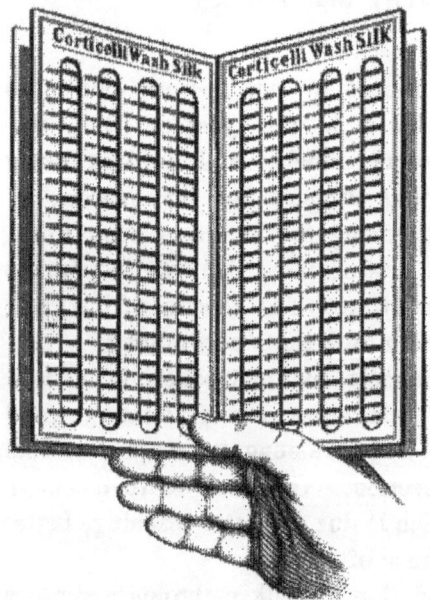

FIG. 1.—COLOR CARD OF CORTICELLI WASH SILK.

The owner of one of these color cards can order by number Corticelli Wash Silk from the storekeeper, either by mail or in person, and in case of failure to obtain what is required, should seek another dealer, or write to the makers, who will see that all orders are filled by some reliable merchant.

Of the seven kinds of silk shown on this card the most useful variety is Filo Silk; being finer than the other kinds, it requires more stitches to cover a given space, and for that reason a skilful worker, with a good selection of colors, produces better results. For small floral designs, and the new jewel patterns, which are now popular, Filo Silk is used exclusively. It is sold in skeins and on spools, and we ask the reader's attention to the latter form, as convenient and economical; the spool protects the silk from injury and enables the worker to cut off quickly (Fig. 2) any length required, avoiding waste and insuring clean, smooth work, with a high lustre. The color number is found on each spool, by which the proper shade is easily selected for any given work, and in any light; the color number is also attached by ticket to all the skein silks under the Corticelli

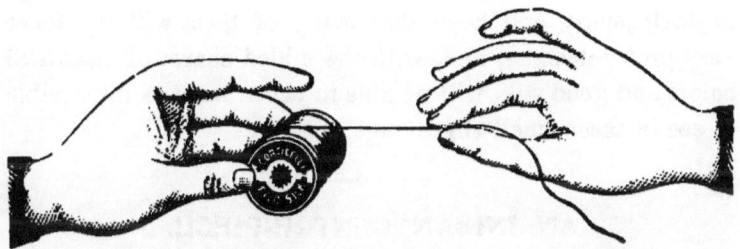

FIG. 2.—SHOWING CONVENIENCE OF SPOOL FOR FILO SILK.

brand. Persian Floss is a new slack-twisted variety lately introduced and is sold in skeins; it is about twice the size of Filo Silk, and is most useful for edges finished in button-hole stitch, and for other purposes. Roman Floss is also a loosely twisted skein silk, coarser than Persian Floss but often used for similar work on heavier material or for bolder patterns. Rope Silk is used for very bold designs on heavy material. In the hands of good artists very rich embroidery is wrought on curtains, counterpanes, cushions and other articles, either with Corticelli Rope Silk or Corticelli Roman Floss.

Some people think that embroidery done in button-hole stitch is more durable and quite as attractive when the harder twisted silk is used, like the EE Embroidery Silk

(Fig. 3) or the Etching Silk; this last kind is also called Outline Embroidery Silk, and it is used for fine outlines of designs, such as stems, tendrils and the conventional ornamental figures so often used by designers in combination with natural flower forms. Corticelli Lace Embroidery Silk in the size No. 500 is now much used for the purpose indicated by its name. This kind of work consists chiefly of button-hole stitch applied to Honiton braid, in the shape of conventional designs executed on linen.

The pieces of embroidery which will be described on the following pages are all worked with some of the kinds of silk we have mentioned. We leave our readers to judge of their merit, and hope that many of them will try these very pretty designs, and, with the added charm of beautiful colors and good silk, will be able to show beauties impossible to see in these small engravings.

AN INDIAN CENTRE-PIECE.

(Figs. 3, 4, 5, 6 and 7.)

This beautiful piece of embroidery is called Indian on account of the colors used for the work, which are like those found in draperies and rugs which are brought from India and other eastern countries.

The materials required are one piece of fine bleached linen twenty-four inches square, ten spools of Corticelli Wash Embroidery Silk, size EE (Fig. 3), white (No. 614), ten spools of Corticelli Filo Silk (Fig. 2) in these washing colors: —

FIG. 3.—CORTICELLI EMBROIDERY SILK FOR BORDER OF FIG. 4.

FLORENCE HOME NEEDLE-WORK.

1 spool No. 736 5, old-blue,
1 spool No. 739, old-blue,
2 spools No 741, yellow,
1 spool No. 742, gold,
1 spool No. 558, old-gold,
2 spools No. 770, burnt-orange,
1 spool No. 774, dull red,
1 spool No. 755, olive-green,

and eight skeins of Corticelli Lace Embroidery Silk, size No. 500, the color being white (No. 614).

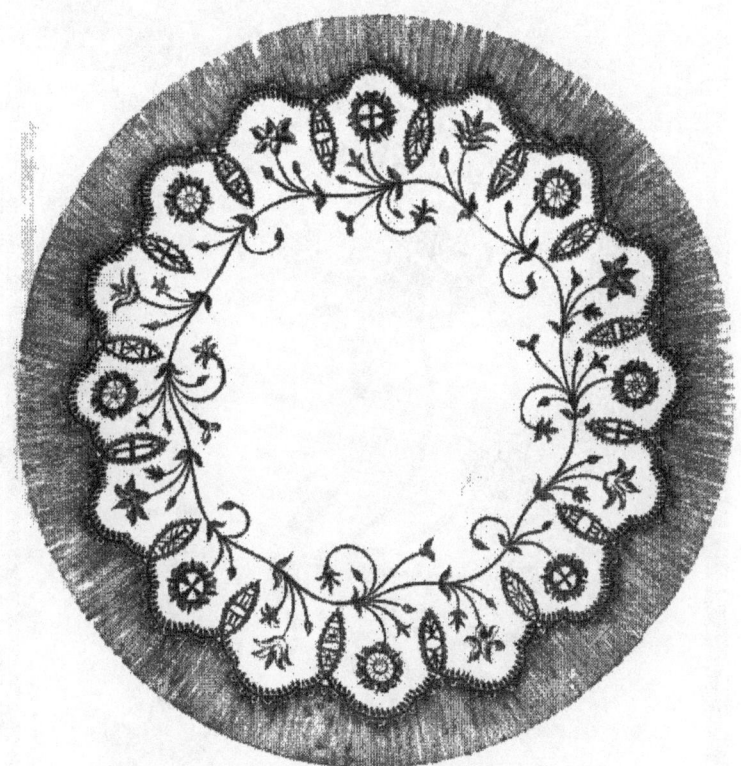

FIG. 4.—INDIAN CENTRE-PIECE.

The scalloped circular border of the design (Fig. 4) is divided into sixteen equal parts, each worked in white with a fancy button-hole stitch, as seen in the engraving; the lace stitches which fill the oval figures and separate the scallops are also worked in white with the EE silk. The fancy button-hole work around each oval is done in white with the size No. 500 silk (which is finer) after the lace stitches are filled in. The round flowers which appear in

FIG. 5.—DETAIL OF FIG. 4.

the conventional wreath have lace-stitch centres worked in white in the same manner as the ovals, the patterns differing, as shown by the engraving. The linen is not cut away behind the lace-filled spaces until after the embroidery is completed. A small hoop should be used while working the lace patterns. The remaining parts of the embroidery which go to make up the design, including flowers, leaves and stems, are worked in Kensington stitch, satin stitch or stem stitch, with Corticelli Filo Silk, using a single thread. The six points of each round flower are old-blue (No. 736.5); the spaces between are first worked solid in yellow (No. 741), being afterwards worked over with scattering stitches of old-gold (No. 558), this shade appearing on the inner half of the circle next to the white button-hole edge. The stems and leaves are worked in one shade of olive-green (No. 755).

A description of Fig. 5 will show the arrangement

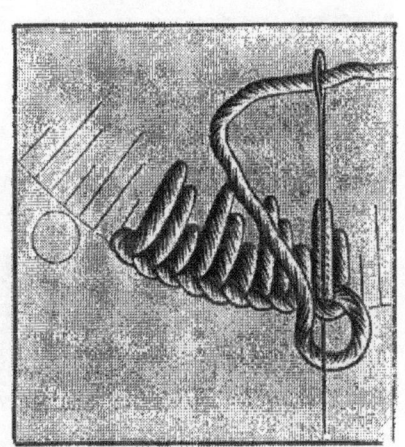

FIG. 9.—DETAIL OF FIG. 4.

of colors in other parts of the design. The two lower petals in the bud shown in lower right-hand corner are worked in olive-green, the next two petals are worked in dull red and the upper petal is worked in lightest yellow. The small bud at left of this group is worked in two shades of old-blue, the darkest shade being used only sparingly at the base. The bud at the extreme left lower corner is worked in two shades of yellow, one petal in the light shade, the next in the darker shade of gold, while the round part connecting with stem is worked in dull red. The bud next above this one is worked in dull red and the one showing four parts, still higher up, is worked in three colors; the lower round spot connecting with stem is dark old-blue, the two next petals are dull red and the upper middle petal is light yellow. The light old-blue, the old-gold and the burnt-orange shades are also used on some of the buds in other parts of the wreath, the seven shades being distributed in a tasteful manner. The full-blown flowers which alternate with those having lace centres are of two kinds, both worked in solid Kensington stitch. The colors used in the one showing six parts are burnt-orange, dull red, light and dark old-blue and light yellow. The upper petal is light old-blue at the top, yellow in the middle and dark old-blue at the base; the other five petals are worked first with the burnt-orange, overlaying that shade at the base of each petal, near the centre of flower, with dull red. A touch of light yellow just under the dark old-blue, on each of the five petals, finishes the flower. There are four flowers worked in this manner.

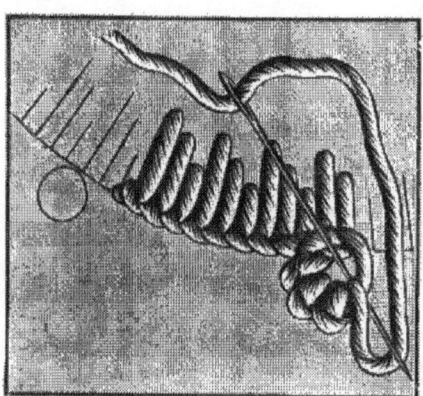

FIG. 7.—DETAIL OF FIG. 4.

The other four full blossoms are worked with burnt-orange, dull red, olive-green and two shades of yellow. The lower part of each flower is worked in olive-green; the middle petal is worked with dull red, streaked afterwards with stitches in two shades of yellow; the other petals are first worked solid with burnt-orange, and then streaked with stitches of dull red and two shades of yellow.

One of the simple but very pretty features of this piece of embroidery is the small projecting "picot" which appears continuously along the button-hole border; each of the sixteen scallops shows seven picots at regular intervals, and the connecting link between the scallops shows one. In order that the manner of making this picot may be clearly understood, the engraver has furnished enlarged cuts, showing the work at two different stages of progress. The first (Fig. 6) shows the fancy indented button-hole edge with the needle passing through the head of the last stitch but one; the thread is drawn through enough to leave a loop into which are to be worked five button-hole stitches, after which — the loop being thus filled — the button-hole work along the edge proceeds until the stamped pattern on the linen shows that it is the place to form another picot. The engraving (Fig. 7) shows but three stitches taken into the loop, but the work is not complete until the space is full, and if the right size of loop is made, five stitches will be enough to fill. It will be necessary to crowd the needle some in forming the last stitch.

This design, stamped on linen, can be obtained in twenty-four inch squares; the instructions printed here are for that size; the measurement refers to the linen, as the design itself is only about twenty-two inches in diameter. Larger squares, suitable for fringing, as shown in engraving (Fig. 4), can also be had. See mention on page 44.

EASTER LILY CENTRE-PIECE.

(Figs. 8, 9 and 10.)

This beautiful example of embroidery is a prize piece which has received the approbation of many competent judges, not only for the needle-work, but for the color scheme, which is white in nearly all parts, including stems and leaves as well as buds and flowers, touches of light green being used only sparingly for tinting on leaves and buds, this color being also used for stamens, which are tipped with yellow.

The materials required are a twenty-two inch square of linen, six skeins of Corticelli Roman Floss, white (No. 615),

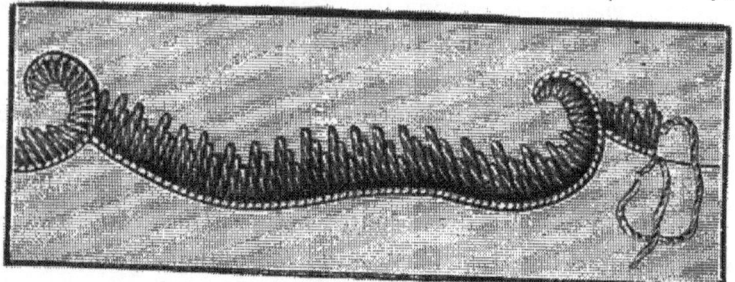

FIG. 5.— DETAIL OF FIG. 10.

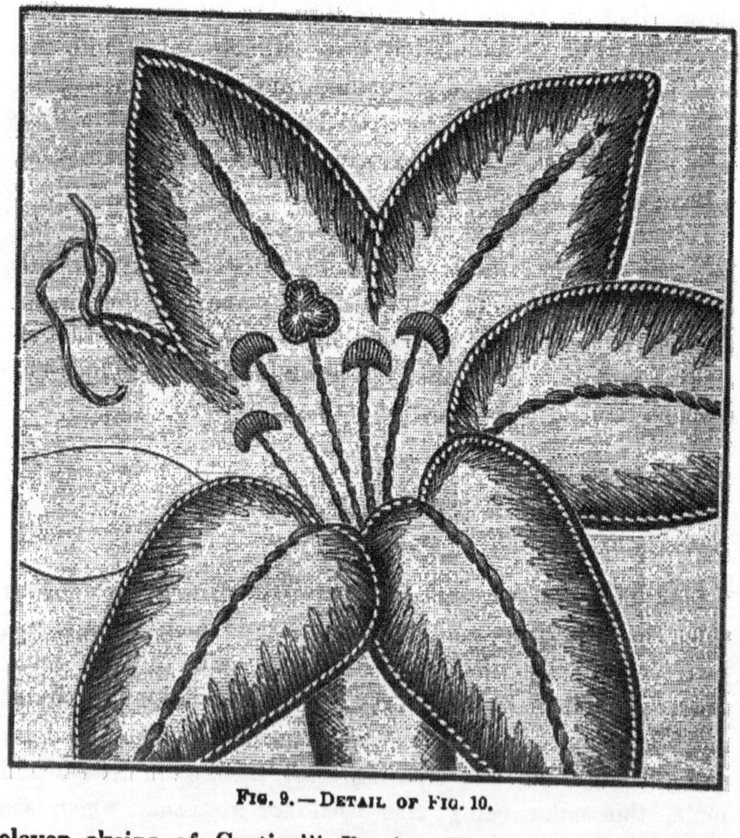

FIG. 9.— DETAIL OF FIG. 10.

eleven skeins of Corticelli Persian Floss, also white, two

yellow (No. 505). The engravings show the work so clearly that description is hardly needed. Fig. 8 shows the border, done in long and short button-hole stitch with white Roman Floss. Fig. 9 shows the full blossom, the petals being worked with white Persian Floss in long and short button-hole stitch, the veins being outlined with the same; the

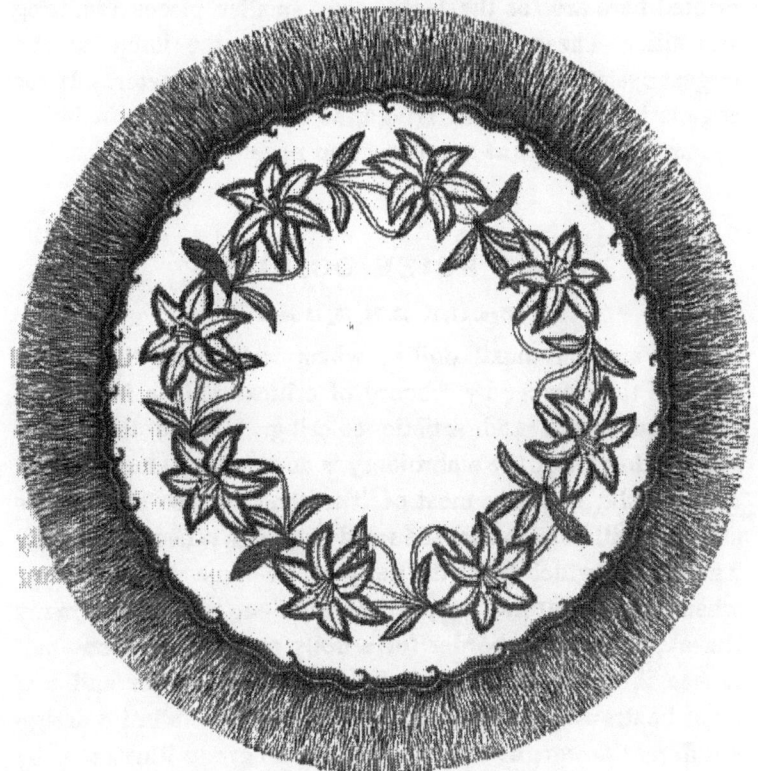

FIG. 10. — EASTER LILY CENTRE-PIECE.

tube is also worked in long and short stitch, but without button-hole work; the stamens are outlined with green and their tips are worked solid with yellow Filo Silk; the pistil is also green, and the tip, which has three divisions, is worked around the edges in button-hole stitch; the leaves are done in long and short stitch with white Persian Floss, at base with green Filo Silk, and the veins are also green; the buds are done in solid Kensington stitch with white Persian Floss, tinted the same as the leaves; the stems are outlined with white Persian Floss.

This design, stamped on linen, can be obtained in twelve, eighteen and twenty-two inch squares. The instructions printed here are for the larger size, smaller pieces requiring less silk. These measurements refer to the linen, as the largest design is only about twenty inches in diameter. If the edge is to be finished in fringe, as seen in Fig. 10, a larger square is required, as mentioned on page 44.

SIX PRIZE DOILIES.

(Figs. 11, 12, 13, 14, 15, 16 and 17.)

Here are six small doilies which well merit the award made to their owner by a board of critical judges for exquisite needle-work and artistic coloring. When it is considered that all of the embroidery is done with a single thread of Filo Silk, and that most of it is done in close button-hole stitch, it will be seen that the word exquisite is used advisedly. The flowers which form the designs are none of them large when in their natural size, but as each one is repeated many times to form the border for a doily only four and one-half inches in diameter, it is obvious that both flower and leaf must be drawn in miniature. Each doily shows in its design a different flower, as will be seen by the group illustrated by Fig. 11, where one doily is seen entire, with five others partially concealed. The list below gives the name of each flower, and the color numbers of the Corticelli Filo Silk used for the embroidery.

Sweet Pea. — Pink, Nos. 572 and 573; green, Nos. 781 and 782.

Orchid. — Yellow, Nos. 741, 742 and 743; green, Nos. 781 and 782; red, No. 544; old-gold, No. 559.

Pansy.— Purple, Nos. 843, 845 and 846 ; green, Nos. 662 and 663 ; yellow, No. 505.

Lily of the Valley.— White, No. 615; green, Nos. 692.9 and 693.

Rose. — Pink, Nos. 572 and 573; old-gold, No. 559; green, Nos. 692.9 and 693.

Bluebell.— Blue, Nos. 518 and 519; green, Nos. 781 and 782.

Only one spool of each shade is required, and this amount is much more than enough, so that in case the prospective worker is pleased to use only one line of green shades, two spools will suffice for six doilies. Our description is given with three different lines of green for the sake of variety.

The six small engravings (Figs. 12, 13, 14, 15, 16 and 17) show sections of the borders in full size, and represent the work in progress. The lightest green silk is used for the button-hole work in all stems, the darker green being used

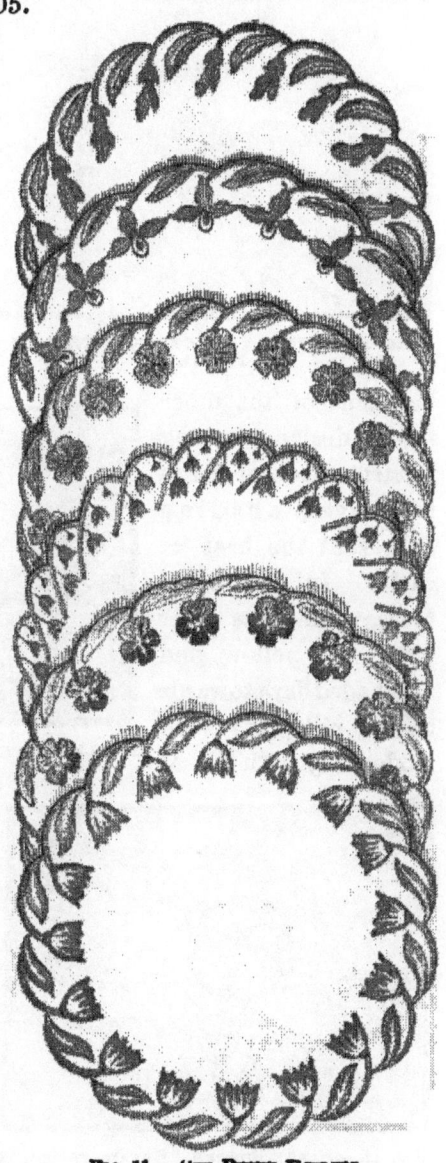

Fig. 11.—Six Prize Doilies.

appears in the drawing. In the design of sweet peas, the leaf is worked in long and short button-hole stitch with light green, shading afterwards with the darker number; the pansy and rose designs are worked in the same way. Satin stitch and Kensington stitch are employed for working the leaves and blossoms of the other three designs, using lightest shade of green for leaves, shading darker at the base of each. In the orchid blossom the three lower petals are yellow, and are shaded dark towards centre, piling the work moderately with silk at that point; the upper part is worked in outline with old-gold, afterwards dotting the enclosed surface with fine darned stitches of red; the silk for this darning should be split, as the spots are very small. The set of prize doilies which was used by our engraver as his models are

FIG. 12.—SWEET PEA BORDER. DETAIL OF FIG. 11.

FIG. 13.—ORCHID BORDER. DETAIL OF FIG. 11.

FIG. 14.—PANSY BORDER. DETAIL OF FIG. 11.

but for lack of space this does not appear in our picture. Either with or without fringe, if the work is well done, the designs are very pleasing.

Seven inch squares of fine bleached linen, stamped with these patterns ready for working, can be obtained through your dealer if you ask him.

Fig. 15.—LILY OF THE VALLEY BORDER. DETAIL OF FIG. 11.

Fig. 16.—ROSE BORDER. DETAIL OF FIG. 11.

See mention of stamped linens on one of the following pages.

Some people think that the difficulty of fringing circular designs like these is great, but this is not the case. After the embroidery is completed on the seven inch square, the corners should be reduced to circular form with a diameter of seven inches, when all the free threads in warp and woof are pulled out, down to the buttonhole edge, after which the small spaces remaining at the corners are easily reduced to fringe by the aid of a pin, when the uneven ends can be

Fig. 17.—BLUEBELL BORDER. DETAIL OF FIG. 11.

EMBROIDERED SOFA PILLOW.

(Figs. 18, 19, 20 and 21.)

A sofa pillow is a pleasing and comfortable addition to the furnishing of a room, especially when made of rich material and well embroidered with silk, using a good design with harmonious colors. Such a design is shown in the engraving

FIG. 18.—SOFA PILLOW DESIGN.

(Fig. 18), which illustrates a square piece of stamped fabric called silk serge. This stuff is lustrous with silk on the surface, which is backed with lisle-thread, to give added strength. The size of the square which we describe here is twenty inches, and the color is called "robin's-egg blue;" on this foundation, the conventional floral pattern, as it appears in the example before us, is very handsome. The details of

the work are shown in Figs 19, 20 and 21, representing sections in full size. It is impossible to show in black and white the full effect of the different shades of olive-green,

FIG. 20.— DETAIL OF FIG. 18.

soft brown and sober red, which are so combined as to give a needle-work picture of rare beauty.

The material used is Corticelli Filo Silk, the entire pattern being worked in Kensington stitch, satin stitch and outline, with a single thread of this silk. The colors required are red (Nos. 769.9, 771, 772 and 774), olive-green (Nos. 662,

664 and 666) and brown (Nos. 778, 779, 525.7, 525.9, 527 and 529). The flowers are done in shades of red in raised satin stitch, using the darkest shade for French knots in centres; the leaves are also worked in satin stitch with shades of olive-green, the darkest green being used for tendrils. Do scrolls and shells with brown, using darkest shade for border.

FIG. 21.—DETAIL OF FIG. 18.

Our readers know the common method of finishing pillow edges with a deep ruffle of soft Japan silk, so that no hemming is required. Such a one was illustrated in "Florence Home Needle-work" for 1895. Brown is a correct color for a ruffle for the pillow we are now considering.

A twenty inch square of blue silk serge, stamped with this design, can be obtained through progressive dealers. See remarks on stamped goods on another page.

EMBROIDERED TEA-CLOTH.

(Fig. 22.)

The common red clover, which grows in great abundance in the fields in many sections of our country, is a pleasing subject for embroidery. It is also the adopted flower of the State

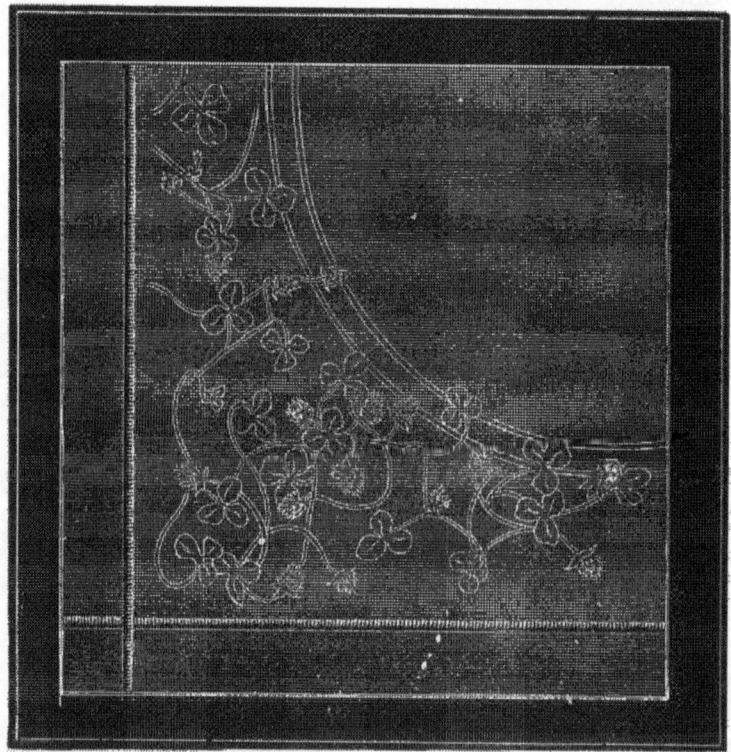

FIG. 22. — EMBROIDERED TEA-CLOTH. CLOVER PATTERN, QUARTER SECTION.

of Vermont, a circumstance which will increase the interest of many persons in the design shown in our engraving. This arrangement of the flower was made for the embroidery on a tea-cloth for Mrs. Kendall, the eminent and gifted English actress, who is now so favorably known to Americans. On her first visit to the United States, upon landing from the clover blossoms, which so pleased her that the flower was afterwards wrought upon her tea-cloth as a pleasant daily reminder of this incident.

The needle-work in the design is done in simple stitches with Corticelli Wash Silk, as follows, viz.: Persian Floss, white (No. 615); Filo Silk, old-pink (Nos. 678, 679, 681, 682), green (Nos. 780, 782, 783, 784). Outline stems with two darkest shades of green Filo Silk; do leaf in four shades of green, using darkest for base and lightest in centre, working in long and short stitch; work the divisions of the flower in solid Kensington stitch in four shades of pink, using the darkest at base. The two circles inside the floral pattern are worked in outline with Persian Floss. The inner circle has a diameter of about twenty inches, the diameter of outer circle being two inches greater. The cloth itself is thirty-six inches square, including a hem of two inches, which is corded on the inner edge and worked over with white silk.

This table cover, with design already stamped, on good bleached linen, with the hem turned and the corded edge worked as described, can be obtained of dealers. Your dealer can get you one if he will; ask him to do so if you like the design. You will be delighted with the simple beauty of the pattern when well worked with correct colors. See reference to stamped linen on another page.

EMBROIDERED TEA-CLOTH.
(Fig. 23.)

The design shown here is made up of butterflies, dragonflies and sprites, arranged in positions both unique and artistic. An unusual opportunity is given to the needle-worker for the play of the imagination in working the sprites, as there is supposed to be no fixed fashion among these creations of the fancy. Nature has also given to the insects a diversity of beautiful colorings, so that each worker is left free to make

28 FLORENCE HOME NEEDLE-WORK.

brilliant hues. We give, in one style, a plan of working, which is done entirely with Corticelli Filo Silk. Blue (Nos. 624, 625, 627), pink (Nos. 535, 536, 536.3), green (Nos. 752.9, 753), black (No. 612), white (No. 615), brown (Nos. 525.9, 526), maize (Nos. 741, 742, 743), salmon (Nos. 534, 715) and yellow (No. 502) are the colors. One spool or skein of each color is more than enough.

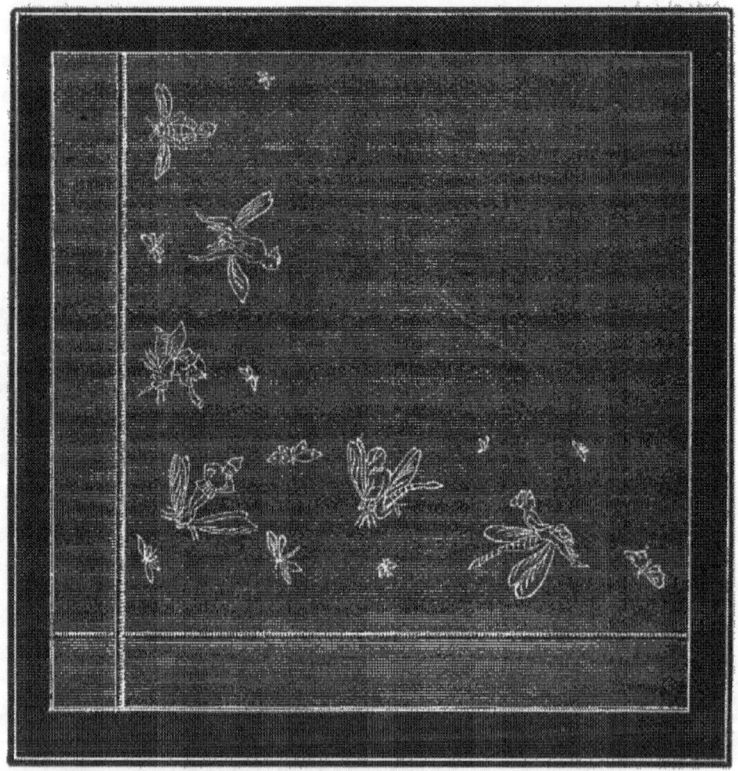

FIG. 23.—EMBROIDERED TEA-CLOTH. BUTTERFLY PATTERN, QUARTER SECTION.

Butterflies. — Work these in outline, using different combinations of color; for instance, work the two back wings in two shades of blue, using the paler for outlines and making veins running from the body in the darker shade; do the two front wings in two or three shades of maize, using the shades. You can use a vein of pale blue with good effect in front wings. The body and feelers are to be worked with dark brown; do the bodies in solid raised work, outlining the feelers with split silk. Work all the butterflies in same way, but in different colors.

If preferred, the wings can be worked with fine effect in Kensington stitch, using light shades on the edges, shading darker towards the body, and veining in a darker or contrasting shade. The bodies must be made either black or brown, and streaked across with maize or yellow.

Dragon-flies.— These creatures are by nature rather sober in color, being dark and inclining to brown and black, yet in the proper light they reflect a brilliant green or yellow, and in working they should be tinted with a light shade of one of these colors.

The Sprites.— Outline the body (face not included) with one thread of silk, working cap in some brighter color; use split Filo Silk for outlining face, making stitches very short. The sprite figures can also be worked solid, the faces only being done in outline. A variety of colors can be used; for instance, work the blouse white, the cap blue and the tights brown. Another good combination is a violet blouse, green tights, cap and feet black, hair black or brown, and face dark flesh-color.

Squares of good linen ready stamped with this design can be obtained of dealers. The size is thirty-six inches, including a hem of two inches, which is corded and nicely overseamed on inner edge of hem with white silk. See reference to stamped linen on another page.

EMBROIDERED TEA-CLOTH.
(Fig. 24.)

This design is a tasteful arrangement of the chrysanthemum and the conventional scroll. The materials for

Filo Silk (Fig. 2), green (Nos. 782, 783 and 785) and yellow (Nos. 740, 741, 742 and 743). Work the scrolls in outline with white, EE, and the flowers and leaves in solid Kensington stitch with yellow and green Filo Silk.

If preferred, old-rose shades (Nos. 715, 716, 717 and 718) may be used for the flowers.

FIG. 24.—EMBROIDERED TEA-CLOTH. CHRYSANTHEMUM PATTERN, QUARTER SECTION.

Ask your dealer to get you a ready stamped cloth like this. The size is thirty-six inches square. The hemming is already done, the inner edge of the hem being over-seamed with white silk. See remarks on stamped linens on another

CHILD'S KNITTED SILK BONNET.
(Figs. 25 and 26.)

The pretty little bonnet seen in Fig. 25 was knit from silk, after a model which belongs to a lady in Virginia, who cherishes it as an heirloom in her family. The original is made of fine linen thread and is a curiosity in knitting, showing much skill in construction. The silk copy which is

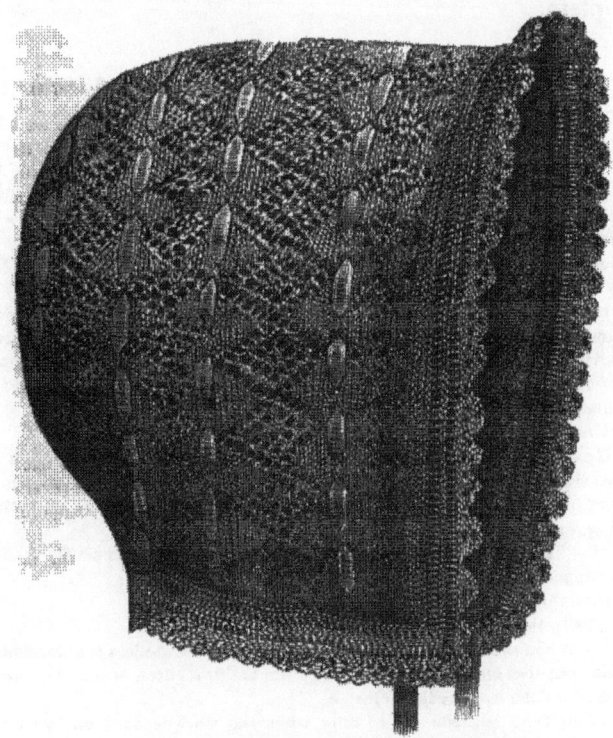

FIG. 25.—CHILD'S KNITTED SILK BONNET.

shown here is made of size No. 500 cream-white Corticelli Knitting Silk, working with five No. 20 needles. One-half ounce (one ball) of this silk is enough for the work; besides this, two yards of narrow white satin ribbon (No. 1) will be needed to run into four rows of the latticed open pattern, as seen in the engraving; one yard of wider ribbon will also be used for ends to tie under chin.

The work begins on the edge in front, and ends in the centre of the crown. It is mostly done in rows, knitting back and forth, but it will be best to divide the stitches (owing to their large number) on four needles, and knit with a fifth. The border, which is knit separately, is sewed on to the edge in front and around the neck after the other work is complete.

EXPLANATION OF ABBREVIATIONS AND TERMS USED.

Cast On.—The best way to form foundation stitches is to knit them on by first forming a tied loop in the silk, slipping it on the left-hand needle; into this loop thrust the right-hand needle, throw thread over, and form a second stitch, which also place on the left-hand needle; into this form another, until the right number is obtained.

K—Means knit plain.

P—Means to purl or seam.

N—Is to narrow, and means to knit two stitches together.

R.N—Means reverse narrowing, and is done by passing two stitches (after knitting) from right to left-hand needle, then with the right-hand needle slipping the second stitch over the first, which is then put back on right-hand needle, thus disposing of one stitch; this has a different effect from ordinary narrowing and is required in some places.

P.N—Means to purl or seam two stitches together.

N.B—Means narrow from the back, that is, thrust the needle into the back loops of the two stitches from right to left, instead of into the front loops the reverse way; this differs from the term pn, the thread being carried in front in that operation, as for purling, but behind for nb, as in plain knitting.

S and B—Is to slip and bind, and means to slip one stitch, knit the next, and pass the slipped stitch over.

O—Means thread thrown over, as if you were about to purl.

S—Is to slip the stitch off without knitting.

Round—When the work is done with four needles or more in a tubular web, this expression describes one circuit of the web from the first stitch of the first needle to the last stitch of the last needle inclusive.

Row.—This term is made use of only when the work is done on two or more needles in a flat web.

Repeat.—This word, following a description of round or row, means that the same work is to be done again, not only once, but throughout the round or row. In other places the word implies a repetition of all rows or rounds preceding it in that rule.

Position of Needles.—The needle where the round begins we style the first; those which follow, the second, third and fourth; and that needle which is out of the work (seldom referred to) we call the fifth. As they are constantly changing places, it is evident that it is the *position* of the needle, rather than the needle itself, which is spoken of.

Cast Off.—This is done by knitting two stitches, passing the first one over the second, and repeating as required.

To knit a stitch crossed is to pass the needle into the stitch on the right-hand side instead of the left, the rest of the operation being the same as knitting plain.

* One or more stars are used, sometimes as a marginal reference, but more frequently they mark a point which is referred to again in the same paragraph or some other rule.

Cast on to 4 needles 231 stitches, and knit as follows:—

1st and 2d rows, knit plain.——3d row, k plain, but in forming each stitch throw thread over 4 times instead of once.——4th row, * slip four loops off as 1 stitch 6 times, which gives you 6 long stitches on the right needle; pass the first 3 of these long stitches over the last 3, placing them all on the left needle; knit the last 3 stitches first, afterwards knitting the first 3, *; repeat from * to * through row.——5th row, knit plain.——6th row, k 5, o twice, n, o twice, n, * k 6, o twice, n, o twice, n, *; repeat from * to * through row, ending with k 5.——7th row, * k 6, k 1 loop, n by knitting togethe. a loop and a stitch from the back, k 1 loop, n from the back, *; repeat from * to * through row, ending with k 4.——8th row, * k 4, o twice, n from the back, k 2, o twice, n, *; repeat from * to * through row.——9th row, k 5, k 1 loop, pn, k 2, k 1 loop, pn, * k 4, k 1 loop, pn, k 2, k 1 loop, pn, *; repeat from * to * through row, ending with k 3.——10th row, k 3, o twice, nb, k 4, o twice, n, * k 2, o twice, nb, k 4, o twice, n, *; repeat from * to * through row, ending with k 3.——11th row, k 4, k 1 loop, pn, k 4, k 1 loop, pn, * k 2, k 1 loop, pn, k 4, k 1 loop, pn, *; repeat from * to * through row, ending with k 2.——12th row, k 3, o twice, n, k 4, o twice, n, * k 2, o twice, n, k 4, o twice, n, *; repeat from * to * through row, ending with k 3.——13th row, n, * k 2, k 1 loop, pn, k 4, k 1 loop, pn, *; repeat from * to * through row, ending with k 2.——14th row, n, k 2, o twice, n, k 2, o twice, nb, * k 4, o twice, n, k 2, o twice, nb, *; repeat from * to * through row, ending with k 3.——15th row, n, k 2, k 1 loop, pn, k 2, k 1 loop, pn, * k 4, k 1 loop, pn, k 2, k 1 loop, pn, *; repeat from * to * through row, ending with k 2.——16th row, n, k 2, o twice, n, o twice, nb, * k 6, o twice, n, o twice, nb, *; repeat from * to * through row, ending with k 3.——17th row, n, k 2, k 1 loop, pn, k 1 loop, pn, * k 6, k 1 loop, pn, k 1 loop, pn, *; repeat from * to * through row, ending with k 2.——18th row, n, knit across plain. You should now have 226 stitches on the needles.——19th row, like third row.——20th row, like fourth row.——21st row, like the fifth row. This completes the first section of the design.——22d row, k 11, o twice, n, * k 10, o twice, n, *; repeat from * to * through row, ending with k 11.——23d row, k 12, k 1 loop, pn, * k 10, k 1 loop, pn, *; repeat from * to * through row, ending with k 10.——24th row, k 10, o twice, nb, o twice, n, * k 8, o twice, nb, o twice, n, *; repeat from * to * through row, ending with k 10.——25th row, k 10, k 1 loop, pn, k 1 loop, pn, * k 8, k 1 loop, pn, k 1 loop, pn, *; repeat from * to * through row, ending with k 9.——26th row, k 9, o twice, nb, k 2, o twice, n, * k 6, o twice, nb, k 2, o twice, n, *; repeat from * to * through row, ending with k 9.——27th row, n, k 10, k 1 loop, pn, k 2, k 1 loop, pn, * k 6, k 1 loop, pn, k 2, k 1 loop, pn, *; repeat from * to * through row, ending with k 8.——28th row, n, k 6, * o twice, nb, k 1, o twice, n, k 1, o twice, n, k 4, *; repeat from * to * through row, ending with k 8.——29th row, k 7, * k 1 loop, pn, k 1, k 1 loop, pn, k 1, k 1 loop, pn, k 4, *; repeat from * to * through row, ending with k 6.——30th row, k 6, * o twice, nb, k 1, o twice, n, o twice, n, k 1, o twice, n, k 2, *; repeat from * to * through row, ending with k 6.——31st row, n, k 5, * k 1 loop, pn, k 1, k 1 loop, pn, k 1 loop, pn, k 1, k 1 loop, pn, k 2, *; repeat from * to * through row, ending with k 5.——32d row,

* to * through row, ending with k 4.——33d row, k 5, * k 1 loop, pn, k 1, k 1 loop, pn, k 2, k 1 loop, pn, k 1, k 1 loop, pn, *; repeat from * to * through row, ending with k 3.——34th row, n, k 1, * o twice, nb, k 1, o twice, nb, k 4, o twice, n, k 1, *; repeat from * to * through row, ending with k 4.——35th row, n, k 3, * k 1 loop, pn, k 1, k 1 loop, pn, k 4, k 1 loop, pn, k 1, *; repeat from * to * through row. ——36th row, k 3, * o twice, n, k 1, o twice, n, k 2, o twice, nb, k 1, o twice, n, *; repeat from * to * through row, ending with k 3.——37th row, n, k 2, * k 1 loop, pn, k 1, k 1 loop, pn, k 2, k 1 loop, pn, k 1, k 1 loop, pn, *; repeat from * to * through row, ending with k 2.——38th row, n, k 2, * o twice, n, k 1, o twice, n, o twice, nb, k 1, o twice, nb, k 2, *; repeat from * to * through row, ending with k 3.——39th row, k 4, * k 1 loop, pn, k 1, k 1 loop, pn, k 1 loop, pn, k 1, k 1 loop, pn, k 2, *; repeat from * to * through row, ending with k 2.——40th row, k 4, * o twice, n, k 1, o twice, nb, k 1, o twice, nb, k 4, *; repeat from * to * through row. ——41st row, n, k 3, * k 1 loop, pn, k 1, k 1 loop, pn, k 1, k 1 loop, pn, k 4, *; repeat from * to * through row, ending with k 3.——42d row, n, k 3, * o twice, n, k 2, o twice, nb, k 6, *; repeat from * to * through row, ending with k 4.——43d row, k 5, * k 1 loop, pn, k 2, k 1 loop, pn, k 6, *; repeat from * to * through row, ending with k 3.——44th row, k 5, * o twice, n, o twice, nb, k 8, *; repeat from * to * through row, ending with k 5.——45th row, n, k 4, * k 1 loop, pn, k 1 loop, pn, k 8, *; repeat from * to * through row, ending with k 4.——46th row, n, k 4, * o twice, nb, k 10, *; repeat from * to * through row, ending with k 5.——47th row, k 6, * k 1 loop, pn, k 10, *; repeat from * to * through row, ending with k 4. ——48th row, knit plain.——49th row, like third.——50th row, like fourth. ——51st row, like fifth.——52d row, k 7, * o twice, n, k 6, *; repeat from * to * through row, ending with k 7.——53d row, k 8, * k 1 loop, pn, k 6, *; repeat from * to * through row.——54th row, k 6, * o twice, nb, o twice, n, k 4, *; repeat from * to * through row, ending with k 6.——55th row, k 7, * k 1 loop, pn, k 1 loop, pn, k 4, *; repeat from * to * through row, ending with k 5.——56th row, k 5, * o twice, nb, k 2, o twice, n, k 2, *; repeat from * to * through row, ending with k 5.——57th row, k 6, * k 1 loop, pn, k 2, k 1 loop, pn, k 2, *; repeat from * to * through row, ending with k 4.——58th row, k 4, * o twice, nb, k 4, o twice, n, *; repeat from * to * through row, ending with k 4.——59th row, k 5, * k 1 loop, pn, k 4, k 1 loop, pn, *; repeat from * to * through row, ending with k 3.——60th row, k 4, * o twice, n, k 1, o twice, n, k 1, o twice, n, *; repeat from * to * through row, ending with k 4.——61st row, k 5, * k 1 loop, pn, k 1, k 1 loop, pn, k 1, k 1 loop, pn, *; repeat from * to * through row, ending with k 3.——62d row, k 5, * o twice, n, k 2, o twice, nb, k 2, *; repeat from * to * through row, ending with k 5.——63d row, k 6, * k 1 loop, pn, k 2, k 1 loop, pn, k 2, *; repeat from * to * through row, ending with k 4.——64th row, k 6, * o twice, n, o twice, nb, k 4, *; repeat from * to * through row, ending with k 6.——65th row, k 7, * k 1 loop, pn, k 1 loop, pn, k 4, *; repeat from * to * through row, ending with k 5.——66th row, k 7, * o twice, nb, k 6, *; repeat from * to * through row, ending with k 7.——67th row, k 8, * k 1 loop, pn, k 6, *; repeat from * to * through row, ending with k 6.——68th row, knit across plain.——69th row, like the third.——70th row, like the fourth.——71st row, like the fifth.——72d row, k 1, * o twice, nb, k 1, o twice, nb, k 2, o twice, n, k 1, o twice, n, *; repeat from * to * through row, ending with o twice, nb, k 1, o twice, nb, k 2, o twice n, k 2.——73d row, k 3, k 1 loop, pn, k 2, k 1 loop, pn, k 1, k 1 loop, pn, * k 1 loop, pn, k 1, k 1 loop, pn, k 2, k 1 loop, pn, k 1, k 1 loop, pn, *; repeat from * to * through row.——74th row, k 3, nb, k 4, o twice, n, k 1, * o twice, nb, k 1, o twice, nb, k 4, o twice, n, k 1, *; repeat from * to * through row, ending with o twice, nb, k 1, o twice, nb, k 5.——75th row, k 6, k 1 loop, pn, k 1, k 1 loop, pn, k 1, * k 1 loop, pn, k 1, k 1 loop, pn, k 4, k 1 loop, pn,

k 1, *; repeat from * to * through row, ending with k 1 loop, pn, k 1, k 1 loop, pn, k 4, k 1 loop, pn, k 2.——76th row, n, k 2, o twice, n, k 2, o twice, nb, k 1, o twice, n, * o twice, n, k 1, o twice, n, k 2, o twice, nb, k 1, o twice, n, *; repeat from * to * through row, ending with o twice, n, k 1, o twice, n, k 2, o twice, nb, k 2.——77th row, n, k 1, k 1 loop, pn, k 2, k 1 loop, pn, k 1, k 1 loop, pn, * k 1 loop, pn, k 1, k 1 loop, pn, k 2, k 1 loop, pn, k 1, k 1 loop, pn, *; repeat from * to * through row, ending with k 1 loop, pn, k 1, k 1 loop, pn, k 2, k 1 loop, pn, k 2.——78th row, n, k 2, o twice, n, o twice, nb, k 1, o twice, nb, k 2, * o twice, n, k 1, o twice, n, o twice, nb, k 1, o twice, nb, k 2, *; repeat from * to *, ending with o twice, n, k 1, o twice, n, o twice, nb, k 2.——79th row, n, k 1, k 1 loop, pn, k 1 loop, pn, k 1, k 1 loop, pn, k 2, * k 1 loop, pn, k 1, k 1 loop, pn, k 1 loop, pn, k 1, k 1 loop, pn, k 2, *; repeat from * to * through row, ending with k 1 loop, pn, k 1, k 1 loop, pn, k 1 loop, pn, k 2.——80th row, n, k 2, o twice, nb, k 1, o twice, nb, k 4, * o twice, n, k 1, o twice, nb, k 1, o twice, nb, k 4, *; repeat from * to * through row, ending with o twice, n, k 1, o twice, nb, k 2.——81st row, n, k 1, k 1 loop, pn, k 1, k 1 loop, pn, k 4, * k 1 loop, pn, k 1, k 1 loop, pn, k 1, k 1 loop, pn, k 4, *; repeat from * to * through row, ending with k 1 loop, pn, k 1, k 1 loop, pn, k 2.——82d row, n, k 3, o twice, nb, k 6, * o twice, n, k 2, o twice, nb, k 6, *; repeat from * to * through row, ending with o twice, n, k 3.——83d row, n, k 2, k 1 loop, pn, k 6, * k 1 loop, pn, k 2, k 1 loop, pn, k 6, *; repeat from * to * through row, ending with k 1 loop, pn, k 3.——84th row, n, k 1, o twice, nb, k 8, * o twice, n, o twice, nb, k 8, *; repeat from * to * through row, ending with o twice, n, k 7.——85th row, n, k 1 loop, pn, k 8, * k 1 loop, pn, k 1 loop, pn, k 8, *; repeat from * to * through row, ending with k 1 loop, pn, k 1.——86th row, n, k 11, * o twice, nb, k 10, *; repeat from * to * through row, ending with o twice, nb, k 11.——87th row, n, k 10, * k 1 loop, pn, k 10, *; repeat from * to * through row, ending with k 1 loop, pn, k 11.——88th row, knit plain.——89th row, like third.——90th row, like fourth.——91st row, like fifth. You have now 204 stitches on four needles; overlap the two edges by 6 stitches and knit 2 together six times, reducing the number to 198; arrange 66 of these on first needle and 44 on each of three other needles, with working thread in last stitch of fourth needle, and knit hereafter in rounds, as follows, viz.:—

1st round, * n, k 20, rn, o twice, *; repeat from * to * through round.——2d round, * k 20, rn, k 1 loop, p 1 loop, *; repeat from * to * through round.——3d round, * n, k 6, o, n, k 9, rn, o twice, n, o twice, *; repeat from * to * through round.——4th round, * k 7, k 1 loop, k 9, rn, k 1 loop, p 1 loop, k 1, k 1 loop, drop 1 loop, *; repeat from * to * through round.——5th round, * n, k 4, o, n, o, n, k 6, rn, o twice, n, k 2, o twice, *; repeat from * to * through round.——6th round, * k 5, k 1 loop, k 1, k 1 loop, k 6, rn, k 1 loop, p 1 loop, k 1, o, n, k 1 loop, drop 1 loop, *; repeat from * to * through round.——7th round, * n, k 4, o, n, k 5, rn, o twice, n, k 1, k 1 loop, k 2, o twice, *; repeat from * to * through round.——8th round, * k 5, k 1 loop, k 5, rn, k 1 loop, p 1 loop, k 5, k 1 loop, drop 1 loop, *; repeat from * to * through round.——9th round, * n, k 8, rn, o twice, n, k 1, o, n, o, n, k 1, o twice, *; repeat from * to * through round.——10th round, * k 8, rn, k 1 loop, p 1 loop, k 2, k 1 loop, k 1, k 1 loop, k 2, k 1 loop, drop 1 loop, *; repeat from * to * through round.——11th round, * n, k 6, rn, o twice, n, k 1, o, n, k 1, o, n, k 2, o twice, *; repeat from * to * through round.——12th round, * k 5, rn, k 1 loop, p 1 loop, k 2, k 1 loop, k 2, k 1 loop, k 3, k 1 loop, drop 1 loop, *; repeat from * to * through round.——13th round, * n, k 2, rn, o twice, n, k 1, o, n, o, n, k 2, o, n, k 1, o twice, *; repeat from * to * through round.——14th round, * k 2, rn, k 1 loop, p 1 loop, k 2, k 1 loop, k 1, k 1 loop, k 8, k 1 loop, k 2, k 1 loop, drop 1 loop, *; repeat from * to * through round. After completing the fourteenth round as described, transfer the extreme right-hand stitch on each of the four needles to the next needle, in order to work the pattern more conveniently later. You have now one stitch on the fourth needle undisposed of, which knit plain, as part of the fourteenth round, and proceed with the next round. —— 15th round, * o twice, n, k 1, o, n, o, n, k 2, o, n, o, n, k 2, rn, *; repeat from * to * through round. —— 16th round, * k 1, p 1, k 2, k 1 loop, k 1, k 1 loop, k 3, k 1 loop, k 1, k 1 loop, k 2, rn, *; repeat from * to * through round. —— 17th round, * o twice, n, k 1, o, n, o, n, k 4, o, n, k 1, rn, *; repeat from * to * through round. —— 18th round, * k 1, p 1, k 2, k 1 loop, k 1, k 1 loop, k 5, k 1 loop, k 1, rn, *; repeat from * to * through round. —— 19th round, * o twice, n, k 1, o, n, k 3, o, n, k 3, rn, *; repeat from * to * through round. —— 20th round, * k 1, p 1, k 2, k 1 loop, k 4, k 1 loop, k 3, rn, *; repeat from * to * through round. —— 21st round, * o twice, n, k 1, o, n, k 3, o, n, k 2, rn, *; repeat from * to * through round. —— 22d round, * k 1, p 1, k 2, k 1 loop, k 4, k 1 loop, k 2, rn, *; repeat from * to * through round. —— 23d round, * o twice, n, k 1, o, n, o, n, k 4, rn, *; repeat from * to * through round —— 24th round, * k 1, p 1, k 2, k 1 loop, k 1, k 1 loop, k 4, rn, *; repeat from * to * through round. —— 25th round, * o twice, n, k 1, o, n, o, n, k 3, rn, *; repeat from * to * through round. —— 26th round, * k 1, p 1, k 2, k 1 loop, k 1, k 1 loop, k 3, rn, *; repeat from * to * through round. —— 27th round, * o twice, n, k 1, o, n, k 4, rn, *; repeat from * to * through round. —— 28th round, * k 1, p 1, k 2, k 1 loop, k 4, rn, *; repeat from * to * through round. —— 29th round, * o twice, n, k 1, o, n, k 3, rn, *; repeat from * to * through round. —— 30th round, * k 1, p 1, k 2, k 1 loop, k 3, rn, *; repeat from * to * through round —— 31st round, * o twice, n, k 1, o, n, k 2, rn, *; repeat from * to * through round. —— 32d round, * k 1, p 1, k 2, k 1 loop, k 2, rn, *; repeat from * to * through round. —— 33d round, * o twice, n, k 1, o, n, k 1, rn, *; repeat from * to * through round. —— 34th round, * k 1, p 1, k 2, k 1 loop, k 1, rn, *; repeat from * to * through round. —— 35th round, * o twice, n, k 3, rn, *; repeat from * to * through round. —— 36th round, * k 1, p 1, k 3, rn, *; repeat from * to * through round. —— 37th round, * o twice, n, k 2, rn, *; repeat from * to * through round. —— 38th round, * k 1, p 1, k 2, rn, *; repeat from * to * through round. —— 39th round, * o twice, n, k 1, rn, *; repeat from * to * through round. —— 40th round, * k 1, p 1, k 1, rn, *; repeat from * to * through round. —— 41st round, * k 1, o, *; repeat from * to * through round. —— 42d round, k 1, and drop loop; draw thread through and fasten.

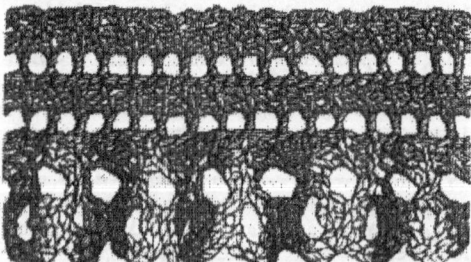

FIG. 26. — KNITTED BORDER. DETAIL OF FIG. 25.

The lace edging which borders the face and neck of this bonnet is made from the same kind of silk and sewed on, rather full; it requires about one yard of the lace for this purpose, which is knit as follows, viz.:—

Cast on 11 stitches, knit across plain. —— 1st row, k 3, o, s and b, k 1, o, s and b, k 1, o twice, k 1, o twice, k 1. —— 2d row, k 2, p 1, k 2, p 1, k 2, p 1, k 2, p 1, k 3. —— 3d row, k 3, o, s and b, k 1, o, s and b, k 7. —— 4th row, cast off 4, k 3, p 1, k 2, p 1, k 3; repeat.

INFANT'S KNITTED SILK SHIRT.

(Fig. 27.)

Materials. — One and one-half ounces Florence Knitting Silk, size No. 300, two No. 16 steel knitting needles and a No. 1 crochet needle. Corticelli Knitting Silk in same size can also be used with satisfaction.

Cast on to one needle 89 stitches and knit across plain. — 2d row, * k 1, o, k 2, s and b, k 2, o, *; repeat from * to * through row, ending with k 1. — 3d row, knit plain; repeat these two rows 13 times more, narrowing one stitch in 29th row,

FIG. 27. — INFANT'S KNITTED SILK SHIRT.

leaving 88 stitches on the needle. — 30th row, * k 2, p 2, *; repeat from * to * through row; turn. — 31st row, same as last row. Continue knitting in 2 and 2 ribs until you have a web ten inches long; then with the first 16 stitches continue knitting in same style two inches more, to form one-half of one shoulder strap; cast off these stitches loosely; also cast off the 56 stitches in the middle of neck; with the

16 remaining stitches, knit two inches more of 2 and 2 ribs, to form one-half of the other shoulder strap, and cast off these stitches loosely; this completes one-half of the knitted part of the shirt. Make another piece in the same way and sew the two together on the sides within three and one-half inches of the top, leaving this space open for the arm-holes; sew also across the top of shoulder straps. The short sleeves are crocheted in the following manner, viz.: do 2 doubles into every third stitch around arm opening, making 24 clusters of doubles in all; do 5 rounds of these doubles, building each cluster of last 4 rounds in the centre of cluster of previous round.——6th round, do 1 slip-stitch into centre of first cluster of doubles in previous round, 6 doubles in centre of next cluster, repeating through round, forming 12 complete shells to finish sleeve. Make spaces around the neck by doing 1 double into about every fourth stitch with 2 chain between; do 1 single into the first space, 6 doubles into second space, repeating throughout round, forming 33 shells to finish. The tasselled cord is crocheted closely from three threads of silk worked together as one; the length should be about thirty-six inches, as the shirt is very elastic and must be drawn on over baby's head; it must be made in two pieces, each beginning at tassel, as follows, viz.: make a chain of 3 stitches and join; then work in rounds, doing 1 single into each of 2 chain and 2 singles into the third; repeat until you have a circle of 7 stitches, then decrease by skipping every third stitch until the number is reduced to one; then continue working in simple close chain stitch until the cord is eighteen inches long; this forms one-half; run this into the spaces from centre of neck to centre of back; make another piece in same way and run into the spaces on the opposite side; join the ends in back of the neck by sewing.

INFANT'S CROCHETED BONNET.

EXPLANATION OF TERMS USED. (Figs. 28, 29, 30, 31 and 32.)

Chain.— This is the first step in crochet, and is explained by Fig. 28, where thread (A) is drawn through loop (B), in direction shown by arrow, until foundation chain is obtained; hence the name. The position of the needle in forming a chain is shown in Fig. 28.

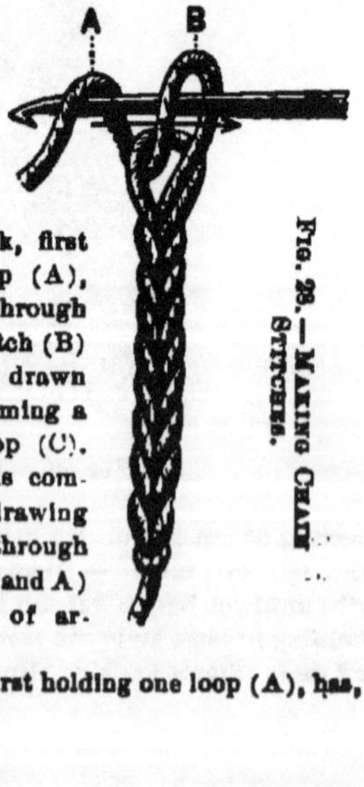

Slip Stitch.— Explained by Fig. 29, where the hook, holding one loop (C), is to be passed in the direction of arrow through stitch (A) of foundation and around thread (B), which is then drawn through stitch (A) and loop (C), leaving a newly formed loop on hook.

Single.— Explained by Fig. 30, where the hook, first holding one loop (A), has been thrust through a foundation stitch (B) and the thread drawn through, forming a second loop (C). The stitch is completed by drawing thread (D) through two loops (C and A) in direction of arrow, again leaving the hook holding one loop.

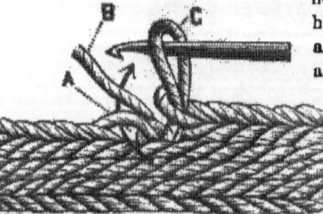

FIG. 29.— MAKING SLIP STITCHES.

FIG. 28.— MAKING CHAIN STITCHES.

Double.— Explained by Fig. 31, where the hook, first holding one loop (A), has, with thread (B) over, been thrust through foundation stitch (C) and thread drawn through, forming another loop (D). With thread (E) over, draw it in the direction of arrow through two loops (D and B), which leaves two loops on hook. Complete stitch by drawing thread through these two loops, which again leaves hook holding a single loop.

Treble. — Made the same as double, except that you pass thread twice around the hook previous to putting it in a stitch, which (counting loop D, Fig. 31) leaves four loops on the needle; you then draw the thread through two loops at a time, putting thread over each time, until one only remains.

Double Treble. — With one loop on the hook and three times thread over, work off the loops by twos, as in a treble.

Materials. — One and one-half ounces (three balls) of No. 300 Corticelli Crochet Silk, two and one-fourth yards of satin ribbon three-fourths inch wide and a No. 1 Star crochet needle. The color of the silk and ribbon is cream-white, shade No. 616.

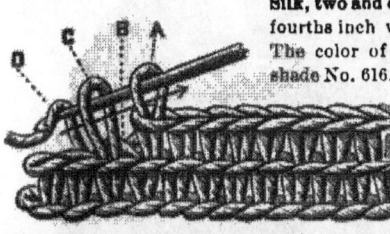

FIG. 30. — MAKING SINGLES.

Make a chain of 7 stitches and join in a ring. — 1st round, do 15 doubles into the ring and join with a slip stitch. — 2d round, widen in every stitch; that is, do 2 doubles into the top of each double of the previous round. — 3d round, do 1 double into top of first stitch, 2 doubles into next; repeat. — 4th round, do 1 double into each of the first 2 stitches, 2 doubles into the next; repeat. — 5th round, do 1 double into each of the first 3 stitches, 2 doubles into the next; repeat. — 6th round, do 1 double into each of the first 4 stitches, 2 doubles into the next; repeat. — 7th round, do 1 double into each of the first 5 stitches, 2 doubles into the next; repeat. — 8th round, do 1 double into each of the first 6 stitches, 2 doubles into the next; repeat. — 9th round, do 1 double into each of the first 7 stitches, 2 doubles into the next; repeat. — 10th round, do 1 double into each of the first 8 stitches,

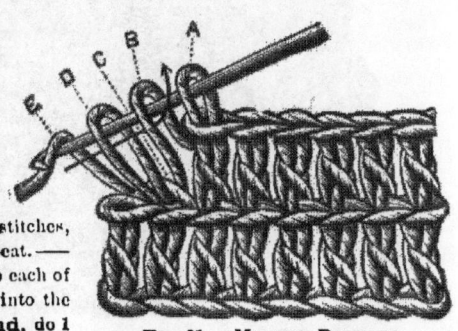

FIG. 31. — MAKING DOUBLES.

2 doubles into the next; repeat. — 11th round, do 1 double into each of the first 9 stitches, 2 doubles into the next; repeat. — 12th round, do 1 double into each of the first 10 stitches, 2 doubles into the next; repeat. — 13th round, do 1 double into each of the first 11 stitches, 2 doubles into the next; repeat. — 14th round, do 1 double into each of the first 12 stitches, 2 doubles into the next; repeat. Break the silk and fasten again in the fifteenth stitch from where the previous rounds began. Do 1 double into the top of every stitch to within 30 stitches from the beginning of this round; turn, and work now in rows back and forth. — 1st row, do 1 double into the top of every stitch. — 2d, 3d, 4th, 5th, 6th and 7th rows, same as first. — 8th row, do 23 chain, fasten in third stitch from the end, * chain 23, fasten 3 stitches further along, *; repeat from

of the first 23 chain of previous row, * chain 3, fasten in twelfth stitch of next 23 chain, *; repeat from * to * throughout row; turn.——10th row, do 1 double into each stitch of last row; turn.——11th row, do 3 chain, 3 doubles into first stitch of previous row, * skip 3 stitches, do 4 doubles into the next, *; repeat from * to * throughout row; turn.——12th row, do 3 chain, 3 doubles into the middle of first shell and 4 doubles into the middle of each other chain shell of previous row; turn.——13th, 14th, 15th, 16th and 17th rows, same as 12th.——18th row, do 23 chain, fasten in fourth stitch from end, * chain 23, fasten 4 stitches further along, *; repeat from * to * throughout row; turn.——19th row, do 12 chain, fasten in the twelfth stitch of 23 chain of previous row, * chain 4, fasten in the

Fig. 32.—INFANT'S CROCHETED BONNET.

twelfth stitch of next 23 chain, *; repeat from * to * to the end of the row; turn.——20th row, do 3 chain, 1 double into each stitch of previous row; turn, and work hereafter in rounds.——1st round, do 3 chain, 3 doubles into first stitch of previous row, * skip 3 stitches, do 4 doubles into next stitch, *; repeat from * to *, placing the shells at regular intervals along the edge of neck and front of bonnet, to form a border.——2d round, do 4 doubles into the middle of each shell of previous round, and also 4 doubles between the shells, which will make the border very full.——3d round, do 4 doubles into the middle of each shell of previous round.——4th round, do 2 doubles into the middle of first shell of previous round, * chain

3, fasten by a single into first stitch of 3 chain, to form a picot, 2 doubles into same shell, chain 3, fasten by a single into first of 3 chain, to form another picot, 2 doubles into middle of next shell,*; repeat from * to * all around the bonnet, which is now ready for the ribbon; run this in under every second loop of the second row and under every second loop of the twelfth row. Crochet a cord of silk and run it in around the neck, to draw that part up if it be too loose. Make a bow for the top and one for the back, as seen in the engraving. Ribbon ties to fasten under the chin complete the work.

Florence Crochet Silk also makes a very pretty bonnet, using the same size and color.

CROCHETED APPLIQUE BORDER FOR A TABLE-COVER.

(Figs. 33 and 34.)

The character of the needle-work in the open border shown in Fig. 33 would hardly be recognized as being done with the crochet needle so closely does it resemble the well-known patterns called drawn-work borders, yet the principal part

FIG. 33.—TABLE-COVER WITH APPLIQUE BORDER, QUARTER SECTION.

of this design is crocheted, embroidery being a minor feature in the decorative scheme. The material used for the lace pattern is No. 500 Corticelli Crochet Silk

(Fig. 34), white (No. 616), and a No. 0 crochet needle. Draw the stitches closely in working.

The insertion for the border is made in separate pieces, one for each side of the square. Make a chain of the required length and proceed in rows, as follows, viz..— 1st row, do 1 treble into the fifth stitch of chain, 1 treble into sixth stitch, keeping the last loop of the trebles on the needle and working them both off together, 2 chain, 1 treble into each of the next 3 stitches, worked in the same way, 2 chain, 1 treble into each of the next 3 stitches, * 9 chain, 1 treble into each of the next 3 stitches, 2 chain, 1 treble into each of the next 3 stitches, 2 chain, 1 treble into each of the next 3 stitches, *; repeat from * to * to the end of the chain; turn.——2d row, do 4 chain, 1 treble into first group of 3 trebles of last row, 2 trebles into next 3 trebles, 2 trebles into next 3 trebles, making 6 in all, keeping the last loop of each treble on the needle and working them off together, * 4 chain, 1 single into fifth of 9 chain of last row, 4 chain, 2 trebles into first 3 trebles, 2 trebles into next 3 trebles, 2 trebles into next 3 trebles, working them all off together, *, repeat from * to * to the end of the row, when you make 4 chain and fasten with a treble into last stitch of last row; turn.——3d row, * do 4 chain, 2 trebles into top of 6 trebles of last row, 2 chain, 2 trebles into same stitch, 2 chain, 2 trebles into same stitch, 4 chain, 1 single into single of last row, *, repeat from * to * to the end of row ; turn.——

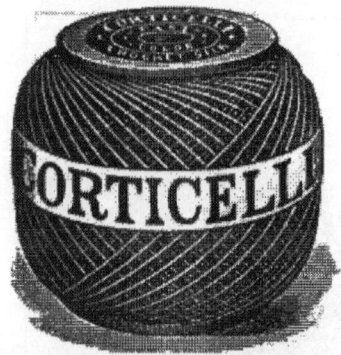

FIG. 34.—CORTICELLI CROCHET SILK FOR APPLIQUE BORDER

4th row, do 4 chain, 2 trebles into first group of 2 trebles of last row, * 3 trebles into next 2 trebles, *; repeat from * to * to the end of row

The spider web in the corner is worked in rounds, as follows 1st round, make a chain of 6 and join in a ring; into this do 32 double trebles.——2d round, do 3 chain, fasten to the end of second row in first piece of insertion, 8 chain, skip 3 stitches, 1 double treble into next stitch, fasten to the end of fourth row of insertion, 8 chain, skip 3 stitches, 1 double into next stitch, 8 chain, skip 3 stitches, 1 double treble into next stitch, 8 chain, skip 3 stitches, 1 double into next stitch, 8 chain, skip 3 stitches, 1 double treble into next stitch, fasten to the end of fourth row in second piece of insertion, 8 chain, skip 3 stitches, 1 double into next stitch, fasten to end of second row in insertion, 8 chain, skip 3 stitches, 1 double treble into next stitch, fasten in the end of chain in both pieces of insertion, to form the corner

The round wheel pattern which appears in the cloth above the border is crocheted in rounds, as follows, viz.: Make a chain of 6 stitches and join in a ring.——1st round, do 16 trebles into the ring, making 3 chain between each treble.——2d round, do 1 single into each loop of 3 chain, with 6 chain between.——3d round, do 1 single into each loop of 6 chain, with 5 chain between.——4th round, do 5 trebles under first 5 chain of last row, keeping the last stitch of each treble on the needle and working them off together, * 7 chain, 5 trebles under next 5 chain, *, repeat from * to *, keeping the last stitch of each treble on the needle and working them off together.——5th round, do 1 single into each loop, with 9 chain between.——6th round, do 1 single into each loop, with 9 chain between.——7th round, do 11 doubles into each loop of last row.

After enough of the insertion is crocheted to surround the cloth, but leaving a space of one inch or more between the hem and the outer edge of the open work, it should be basted on to the right side squarely, as seen in the engraving, and then closely button-hole stitched around the inner and the outer edges with the same kind of silk. After thus securing the silk insertion firmly to the linen, that portion of the latter which is between the button-holed edges is cut away with sharp-pointed scissors, leaving an open pattern of great beauty. Fancy embroidery stitches are then worked around the upper edge. The crocheted figure above the border is applied to the linen in the same manner as is the insertion. A row of fancy embroidery stitches is afterwards worked around the outer edge of the circle.

One-half ounce (one ball) of the silk is enough for all the needle-work.

This cloth is thirty-six inches square, including a two-inch hem, which is neatly over-seamed with white silk.

Linen squares hemmed in this way, but with plain centres suitable for this kind of work, can be obtained through dealers. See reference to stamped linens on another page.

NEW COLORS IN CORTICELLI SILK.

The embroidery designers are constantly introducing new flowers and other objects of ornament for conventional treatment into their work, making changes of color and shadings necessary to meet their requirements. The makers of Corticelli Silk are quick to produce these in permanent dyes, and have recently made a thorough revision of their color card, greatly improving old and standard shadings, and adding a large number of new lines, so that their latest one shows more than three hundred separate and distinct shades.

For the benefit of our readers we give below a list of the improved shadings, and also another list, showing the new lines as they appear on a color card which we have before us; we advise every one who does embroidery to procure one of these late cards.

The improved shadings are as follows, viz.: —

Nos. 511 to 515, lavender to purple.	Nos. 688.9 to 692, wood-brown.
Nos. 534 to 544, pink to red.	Nos. 692.8 to 696, olive.
Nos. 548.5 to 556, green.	Nos 725 to 729.5, violet.
Nos. 557.9 to 561, olive-bronze.	Nos. 744 to 749.5, bluette to Yale blue.
Nos. 635.5 to 640, old-pink.	Nos. 760 to 769, pink to scarlet.
Nos. 649.9 to 655, lilac to red purple.	Nos. 780 to 785, olive.

Nos. 786 to 796, Delft blue.

The new lines of colors are all good, and appear under these names and with the following numbers, viz.: —

Nos. 684 to 688, olive-green.	Nos. 821 to 825, Delft blue.
Nos. 797 to 802, nasturtium yellow.	Nos. 826 to 830, sea grass (red.
Nos. 803 to 808, Empire green.	Nos. 831 to 838, apple-green.
Nos. 809 to 820, nasturtium.	Nos. 839 to 842, slate.

Nos. 843 to 848, pansy (purple).

READY STAMPED DESIGNS

ON LINEN AND SILK SERGE.

If you are a reader of "Florence Home Needle-work" and are pleased with the designs which are shown on a small scale in this publication, you may wish to obtain some of them ready stamped on good linen. If so, go to your dealer and show him the pictures; he may have the very pieces you want, as well as Corticelli Silk for working them, but if not, and he is an enterprising man, he will probably get them for you from one of our agents in the large cities.

If you cannot conveniently secure the designs in this way, write to us and we will cause them to be sent to you through a reliable party in our locality on receipt of the price named in the list below.

In ordering, do not forget to mention the size, as well as the style or design, as described. The dimensions spoken of refer to the fabric and not to the design; a square of linen which measures twenty-two inches usually has a design which is one and one-half inches less in diameter.

All of the linen offered here is of the fine bleached variety.

PRICE LIST.

Stamped Linen, 27 inches square, with margin for fringe outside the design, Figs. 4 and 10, ... $0.60 each.
Stamped Linen, 24 inches square, Fig. 4, ...50 "
Stamped Linen, 22 inches square, Figs. 10, 36, 39, 40, 41, 42, 43, 44, 45, 46, 47, 48, 49, 51, 52, 53, 54, 55, 57, 58, 59, 60, 61, 62 and 63, ...40 "
Stamped Linen, 18 inches square, Figs. 10, 36, 39, 40, 41, 42, 48, 44, 45, 46, 47, 48, 49, 51, 52, 53, 54, 55, 57, 58, 59, 60, 61, 62 and 63, ...30 "
Stamped Linen, 12 inches square, Figs. 10, 36, 39, 40, 41, 42, 43, 44, 45, 46, 47, 48, 49, 56, 57, 58, 59, 60, 61, 62 and 63, , ...15 "
Stamped Linen, 9 inches square, Figs. 36, 49, 57, 58, 59, 60, 62 and 63, . .12 "
Stamped Linen, 7 inches square, Figs. 11, 62 and 63, ...10 "
Stamped Linen, 6 inches square, Figs. 11, 62 and 63, ...08 "
Stamped Silk Serge, 20 inches square, Fig. 18, ... 1.00 "
Stamped Linen Tea-cloth, 36 inches square, hemstitched and with silk corded edge, Figs. 22, 23 and 24, ... 1.50 "
Plain Linen Tea-cloth, 36 inches square, hemstitched and with silk corded edge for crochet-applique design, Fig. 33, ... 1.50 "

Nonotuck Silk Co.,
FLORENCE, MASS.

SILK JEWELS IN EMBROIDERY.

(Figs. 35, 36, 37 and 38.)

BEAUTIFUL imitations of the precious stones, wrought with silk, are a prominent feature in embroidery at the present time, the marvellous lustre of Corticelli Filo Silk (Fig. 35), with its brilliant and tenacious dyes, making it possible to faithfully reproduce the shapes and colors of nearly all of the well-known gems, the diamond only defying the art of the dyer and the needle-worker; the amethyst, the emerald, the garnet, the pearl, the opal, the ruby, the sapphire, the turquoise and other stones finding their proper hues among the colors of this beautiful silk.

This style of embroidery was undoubtedly suggested by the needle-work of Oriental countries as practised in early days, — and perhaps at the present time, — in which, mingled with complicated stitches done in brilliant colored silk, are often found real gems, or their counterfeits in paste or glass. The silk jewel has almost the same effect as these, when well made, and has the advantage of being light and durable, as well as inexpensive; it can be placed on white linen or other material which may require washing.

FIG. 35. — CORTICELLI FILO SILK FOR JEWELS.

The jewel designs which are illustrated here consist of circular patterns called centre-pieces, and they can be obtained ready stamped in a number of sizes. As will be seen by the engravings, the jewels are clustered or otherwise placed in such artistic manner as will best display an harmonious color effect, and the beauty of any jewel design is dependent on this. The patterns shown admit of various kinds of treatment, as will be seen by the descriptions which follow, and the same design may be wrought in several ways. The forms of the jewels as used in embroidery are usually round or oval, the size being adapted to the design. The material on which the work is done should be held in a hoop to keep it firm. The space to be covered is first darned thickly over with cotton floss or raw silk, which is still better, building up high towards the centre to form a solid and true convex surface, the highest point being in the centre; this is called padding, and it is necessary, for the best result, to lay these foundation stitches exactly at right angles to those which are afterwards worked with the Corticelli Filo Silk, in the color of the gem desired. Lay the silk very evenly and closely, as illustrated in Fig. 37, which shows the work in several stages of progress, some jewels being complete. For the convenience of our readers a list of the proper colors for the best known precious stones is furnished.

FIG. 36.—JEWEL DESIGN.

CORRECT COLORS FOR PRECIOUS STONES AS USED IN JEWEL EMBROIDERY.

Amethyst. — Purple, Nos. 649.9, 650 and 651.
Emerald. — Green, Nos. 548.5, 549, 550 and 551.
Garnet. — Red, Nos. 540, 541 and 542.
Opal. — Violet, No. 725; green, No. 692.8; pink, No. 678, and blue, No. 735.5, are the colors seen in this peculiar gem. The silk can be split, thus securing a closer shading to produce an irridescent effect if care is exercised; the lightest tint appears in centre and darkest on edge. When outlined with pale green the imitation is nearly perfect.
Pearl. — White, No. 614.
Ruby. — Red, Nos. 655.9, 656, 657, 658 and 659.
Sapphire. — Blue, No. 749.
Topaz. — Yellow, Nos. 644.7, 644.8, 644.9 and 645.
Turquoise. — Blue, Nos. 623 and 624, or Nos. 520 and 521.

Other pale colors are employed in jewel work, such as Nos. 780, 781, 752.9, 692.9, 699, 519, 750, 803 and 831; for the outline stitches, which are worked around some of the forms, metallic yellows are used, representing gold settings; Nos. 525.7, 525.8, 644.7, 644.8 and 644.9 are good for this purpose.

The engravings shown here represent some jewels outlined in close stitches surrounding the raised centre; this outline is sometimes worked in the same color and shade, in other cases a darker shade is used; other jewels are seen which have no outline, but which are raised high. In cases where the padding is very slight, the addition of a dark outline gives the centre the effect of being high, and this is often desirable, especially with large jewels. Another treatment which is very effective is to outline the raised jewels with a shade of yellow which imitates a gold setting, and this is more particularly true of gems which are not yellow, on account of greater contrast.

An examination of illustrated jewel patterns and descriptions which follow will show examples of these different applications.

The design seen in Fig. 36 shows a pleasing and brilliant example of jewel work. It requires for working the following kinds of silk, viz.: three skeins of Corticelli Roman Floss, white, 615, and two of yellow, 742; nineteen spools of Corticelli Filo Silk are also used, two purple, 650, three pink, 637, one brown, 525.9, two blue, 623, one red, 768, two green, 781, one yellow, 741, four yellow, 742, two yellow, 743, and one white, 615.

Fig. 37.—DETAIL OF FIG. 36.

The following brief description tells where to place the colors. The color numbers are now found on the end of each spool of this silk, a convenience our readers will appreciate.

Border.—Button-hole stitch the four scallops below the parallel lines with Roman Floss in white; work these lines above the scallops with yellow Filo Silk, 742, filling in the space between with the same silk in fine French knots. The crescent-shaped loops which connect the scallops are raised with cotton or raw silk, being afterwards worked with white Filo Silk. Button-hole stitch the edges of the five-leaved

FIG. 38.—DETAIL OF FIG. 36.

rosette between the large scallops with Roman Floss in yellow, 742; work in space inside each leaf, as far back as shown by stamping, with Filo Silk in three shades of yellow, the light shade being used nearest the outer edge, shading

Silk in red, and the eight smaller jewels of same group with alternate shades of purple and green.

Jewelled Clusters. — Work the eleven oblong jewels in one cluster with Filo Silk in blue, and the next cluster with pink; work the seven small jewels inside the first group with Filo Silk in brown, and those in the next group with Filo Silk in green. Repeat this order all around. The six jewels which appear in each scallop between the lines are purple amethysts. Outline all the jewels with their own color, raising them.

This design is made in four sizes, twenty-two, eighteen, twelve and nine inch squares.

These instructions are for size twenty-two; smaller pieces take less silk.

PRACTICAL PATTERNS FOR JEWEL EMBROIDERY.

(Figs. 39, 40, 41, 42, 43, 44, 45, 46, 47, 48 and 49.)

These designs can be obtained in three different sizes, stamped on linen squares measuring twenty-two, eighteen and twelve inches each. The diameter of a pattern is less by about one and one-half inches than the square of linen.

In all the descriptions which follow the material used for embroidery is either Corticelli Roman Floss, Corticelli Persian Floss or Corticelli Filo Silk. The first two are coarse and medium sizes used for the borders; the last is fine and is used exclusively for jewels and other work within the borders.

The numbers are taken from the Corticelli color card. We do not think it advisable to try to name the amount of silk required for each pattern, but it is well to know that a design which is twenty inches in diameter (the square of linen for this is called twenty-two inches) will require about six skeins of Roman or Persian Floss for the border, and that smaller pieces will take less silk; for the jewels and other work, in many cases only a single spool or skein of Filo Silk will be needed in each shade.

Most of the designs are worked in outline, introducing a moderate amount of solid work on points and elsewhere for good effect. The jewels are all padded either with white cotton floss or raw silk before covering with the Filo Silk in the proper colors as directed.

It is best to launder your embroidery if soiled before cutting away cloth around the design.

FIG. 39.—JEWEL DESIGN.

JEWEL DESIGN (Fig. 39). *Material.*—Persian Floss, white, 614; Filo Silk, blue, 623; yellow, 740, 741, 742; maize, 645; green, 661, 665. *Border.*— Work scallops in indented button-hole stitch, slightly padded, with white Persian Floss; outline the inner edge of each scallop with pale green Filo Silk and do the border jewels in blue. *Flower.*—Work in button-hole stitch with shades of yellow, lightest on edges and dark towards base; do the jewel in centre with maize; outline cross-bars with lightest green and cross-stitch with dark green.

JEWEL DESIGN (Fig. 40). *Material.*— Persian Floss, white, 614; Filo Silk, yellow, 741, 742, 743; maize, 645; olive, 662, 663, 665; green, 548.5; old-pink, 679. *Bor-*

der. — Work scallops between flowers with white Persian Floss in button-hole stitch; the five petals which show also in the border, as well as those above, do with Filo Silk in three shades of yellow, worked in long and short button-hole stitch; work the jewels in centre of flower with maize, not outlined. *Jewels and Leaves.* — Work jewels next border with emerald green, not outlined; do lower chain of pearls in white, outlined with medium olive, and upper chain in old-pink, outlined also with olive; work the oval jewel in cluster with pale olive, and those surrounding it with purple, each outlined with self shade; work the spray of leaves with shades of olive, using darkest at bottom and for stems; the connecting links between the pearls should be medium olive.

Fig. 40. — Jewel Design.

Jewel Design (Fig. 41). *Material.* — Persian Floss, white, 614; Filo Silk, green, 752.9, 753, 754; pink, 657; gold, 644.8; brown, 619, 620, 622. *Border.* — Work scallops solid with white Persian Floss, using padded button-hole stitch on inner circle and long and short button-hole stitch on the leaves; after working these in white, shade inside with green filo, placing darkest at base; a pink jewel looks well at this point though the stamped pattern does not show it. *Medallion.* — Work leaves in long and short stitch in shades of green, using darkest at base; do jewels in pink, set in gold; outline medallion frame in brown, using third shade outside, second shade inside, and the first or lightest shade for strokes between.

JEWEL DESIGN (Fig. 42). *Material.*—Persian Floss, green, 781; Filo Silk, green, 782, 783, 784; pink, 678, 679; white, 614; maize, 644.7, 645; old-blue, 737; red, 540. *Border.*—Work in solid padded button-hole stitch with green Persian Floss. *Jewels and Flowers.*—Work the jewels in border with red Filo Silk set in gold; do the strings of jewels alternating white and light pink, outlining with light green and using that color for connecting cord; work the large jewel in

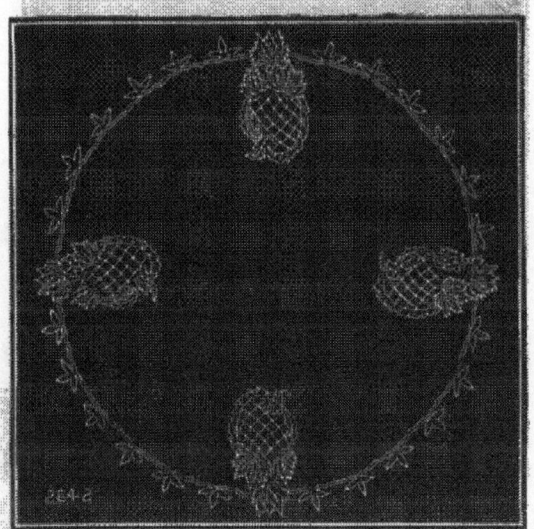

FIG. 41.—JEWEL DESIGN.

cluster between chains with old-blue set in gold, and the small ones with second shade of maize, not outlined; work the jewels in the flower in second shade of pink, outlining with the same; do the petals of flower in shades of green, working in long and short button-hole stitch; do the crosslines in centre in outline with dark green.

JEWEL DESIGN (Fig. 43). *Material.*—Persian Floss, white, 614; Filo Silk, green, 692.9, 693, 694; purple, 650; pink, 657; gold, 644.9; white, 614. *Border.*—Work scallops in long and short button-hole stitch with white Persian Floss, padding the edge slightly.

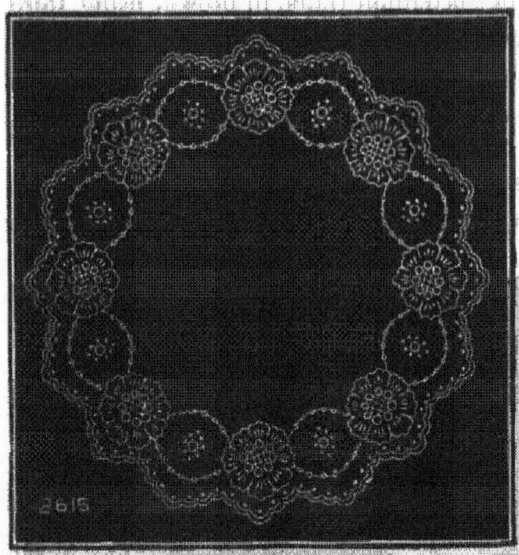

FIG. 42.—JEWEL DESIGN.

Jewels.—Work small ones near border with Filo Silk in purple, without outline; do those in the medallion with pink, outlined in same color, those between lines with gold, not outlined; for the cluster of jewels near the point of scallop use purple for centre; do the small ones in this group in pale green; for the clusters on either side use second shade of green for centre and purple for small ones; for the cluster above the lines use purple for large stone and white for small ones; outline each clustered jewel with it own color, with the exception of the pearls, which are white and should be set in second shade of green.

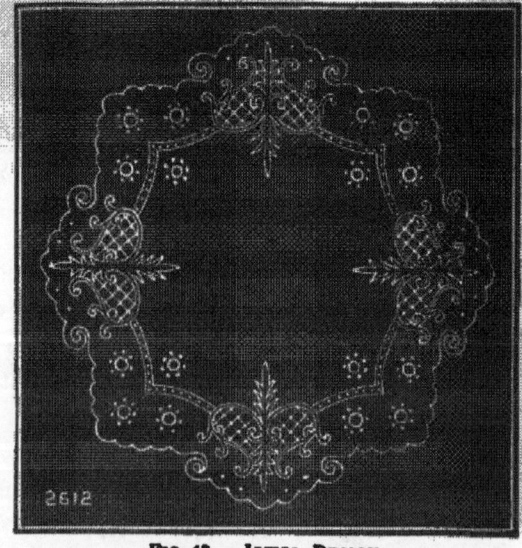

FIG. 43.—JEWEL DESIGN.

Scrolls.—Work with shades

of green touched up with white on points, using darkest green towards the centre; the work can be done mostly in outline, using long and short stitches on points to give the pattern better effect; do cross-bars in palest green outline.

JEWEL DESIGN (Fig. 44). *Material.*— Persian Floss, white, 615; Filo Silk, white, 615; green, 783; blue, 626; red, 540; gold, 644.8. *Border.*—Work centre of large scallop with white Persian Floss in padded button-hole stitch, do outer edge of scroll on each side in narrow button-hole stitch, also white; outline the inner edge of border scrolls with green Filo Silk, using long and short stitches on points. *Scrolls and*

FIG. 44.—JEWEL DESIGN.

FIG. 44.—JEWEL DESIGN.

Jewels. — Work jewelled scroll in outline, using white Filo Silk and making points heavy with long and short stitches; do both round jewels in red, outlined with gold, and the nine jewels above in blue, also set in gold; work the alternate scroll in same way, using white silk for all parts, and touching up with green on points; use padded satin stitch in green for the cross-band.

JEWEL DESIGN (Fig. 45). *Material.* — Persian Floss, white, 614; Filo Silk, red, 656, 658, 660; green, 548.5; blue, 623, 626; white, 614; gold, 644.9. *Border.* — Work scallops and scrolls in solid button-hole stitch with white Persian Floss. *Jewels.* — Work large jewel in cluster with darkest blue set in gold; do next two in yellow outlined with same, and next two in green set in gold, with lower one red, also set in gold; do small jewels on either side in light blue; work the jewels in festoons in three shades of red, the smallest being light and largest dark, outlining in same shades. *Scrolls.* — Work in shades of green in outline, but using long and short stitches on points; outline spaces in bottom of festoons with dark green and fill with fancy stitches in white.

FIG. 46.—JEWEL DESIGN.

JEWEL DESIGN (Fig. 46). *Material.* — Persian Floss, white, 615; Filo Silk, green, 833, 834 and 835; purple,

726, 727 and 729; maize, 644.7, 644.9, 646. *Border.* — Work scallops in padded solid button-hole stitch with white Persian Floss; do border jewels with darkest green outlined with first shade of maize. *Flower.* — Outline edge between the jewels with second shade of green; work large jewels in each alternate group with first shade of maize and medium jewels with second shade; do round jewels in centre with third shade of purple; do the jewels in the next flower in same way, but using light and medium purple for outer jewels and dark maize for round jewels in centre. *Scroll.* — Do this in outline with darkest green.

JEWEL DESIGN (Fig. 47). *Material.* — Persian Floss, yellow, 501, 502; Filo Silk, purple, 650; red, 658; olive, 663; green, 548.5; gold, 644.8; blue, 626.

FIG. 47.—JEWEL DESIGN.

Border. — Work seven outer parts of scallop in indented button-hole stitch with first shade of yellow Persian Floss, and the five other parts above in same way with the second shade; outline the inner boundary of these figures in olive Filo Silk. *Jewels.* — Work large round ones nearest edge in red and the small ones near by in blue; do the oval jewel in cluster with purple and the small ones which surround it with green; pad all the gems, and give them a good gold setting; the indented work in border will also look well if slightly padded on edge.

JEWEL DESIGN (Fig. 48). *Material.* — Persian Floss, white, 614; Filo Silk, green, 781, 782, 784; red, 658; white, 614; blue, 626; pink, 656. *Border.* — Work middle scallops in solid button-hole stitch with white Persian Floss; do fan-shaped figure in long and short button-hole stitch with same, tinting with green Filo Silk back of the white; do the jewel at base of fan with red, 658; work string of pearls with white, outlining with light green, and connecting cord with same shade of green. *Medallion.* — Work scrolls in shades of green in outline with long and short stitch on points

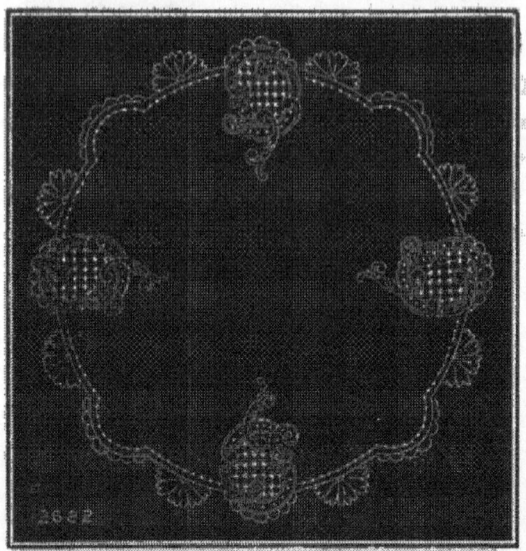

FIG. 48. — JEWEL DESIGN.

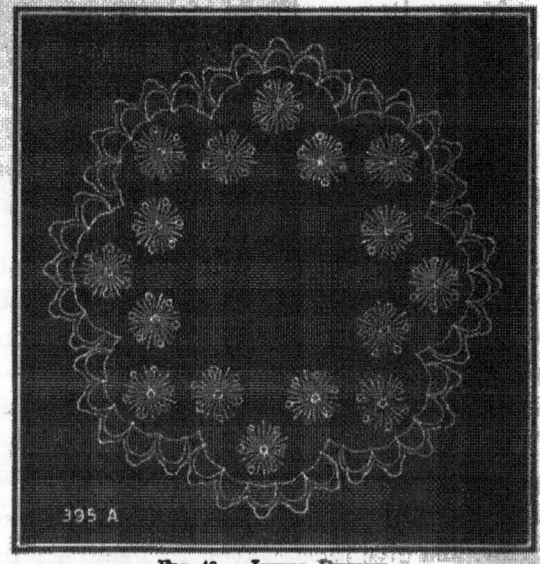

FIG. 49. — JEWEL DESIGN.

in lightest shade; do cross-bars in first shade of green

again crossed with blue; work jewels in medallion frame with pink.

JEWEL DESIGN (Fig. 49). *Material.* — Roman Floss, green, 663; Filo Silk, yellow, 504, 506; green, 692.8, 663. *Border.* — Button-hole stitch the lower part of scallops with green Roman Floss, using same shade to work outline above; fill the space between with fancy stitches, either star stitch, double-cross stitch or lace work, using the dark yellow Filo Silk. *Jewels nearest Scallop.* — Work alternate jewels in light and dark yellow Filo Silk, first working over the spaces in opposite way with cotton or raw silk to raise them; outline around the edge of each jewel with same color. *Outspreading Rays.* — Work the long one, and each alternate, in feather stitch with darkest green; outline the intermediate rays with the lightest green. This is for the clusters of yellow jewels; reverse the colors and work the outspreading rays between the green jewels with two shades of yellow. *Inside Row of Jewels.* — Work each alternate jewel with light green and each intermediate with dark green, raising as before.

MARKING CLOTHING.

Every housekeeper should mark plainly all her sheets, pillow-cases, towels, napkins, tablecloths and white spreads. They are very apt to be lost when not so marked, being misplaced and mistaken for the property of other people in the laundries. Personal wardrobe should also be marked, for the great convenience of all who handle the numerous handkerchiefs, stockings, shirts, collars and cuffs which go to make this up. It is convenient and rapid to mark with a pen with Payson's Indelible Ink. A bottle of this should be found in every house, and it is a good idea to keep on hand a few yards of linen tape, on which is written, with this ink, many times over, your name. The tape can then be cut in pieces, which are ready to sew on to stockings and other articles having too rough a surface for pen work. "Marking should not be left to laundries and their cheap inks and coarse cabalistic characters; much disfigurement and injury to fabrics and marking often ensue when strong chemicals are used, with these inferior inks; it is best, therefore, to do your own marking with that reliable brand known for over sixty years as Payson's." The marking can also be effectively done with Corticelli Wash Silk, in any color, by those handy with the needle.

SOME SELECTED DESIGNS

FOR

CENTRE-PIECES AND DOILIES.

HE selection of a pattern for embroidery is difficult for some people, owing to the bewildering variety of subjects which are offered by dealers. It is to be regretted that some of the designs are not of a character to encourage progress in fine art needle-work, but good ones are to be had, and it is our purpose to illustrate and describe briefly some of these which are meeting with favor among good workers. Floral patterns are favorites, while fruit and conventional pieces find many admirers; all find places in our descriptions.

One good design successfully carried out will create a desire in the ambitious worker to do other and more difficult work, until, with practice, nothing will be considered beyond her ability.

Special attention is called to the first five floral patterns, which have borders alike but which are intended for different color treatment. These descriptions are written after seeing examples of the work of exceptional beauty. It is to be regretted that space forbids showing them in full size, with details of stitches. The scrolls are designed for heavier work than that which is used for the small field flowers, which peep modestly out from underneath, as if suggesting the contrast between them and the showy garden flowers which hold a more conspicuous position within the border.

The rose and the carnation are popular flowers and have the advantage of brilliant hues in some varieties, but the white syringa, with its tinted petals and stamens, when placed within a border of small flowers, also tinted with green and yellow, rivals them in modest beauty.

The other floral designs, as well as the fruit and conventional patterns, are good and have practical descriptions. Linen squares showing these patterns in several sizes can be obtained through dealers. See remarks on this subject on other pages.

A PADDED BORDER (Fig. 50). *Material.*—Persian Floss, white, 614; Filo Silk, purple, 651; green, 548.5; raw silk,

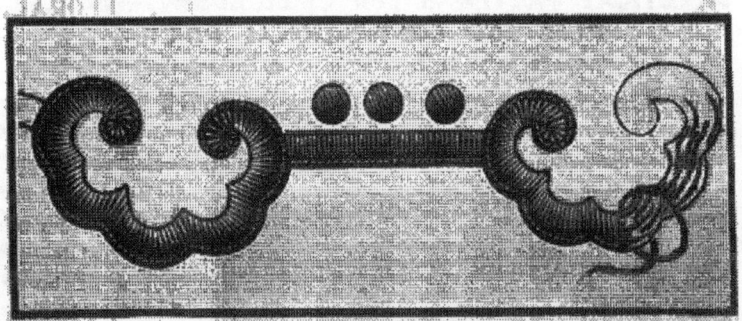

FIG. 50.—A PADDED BORDER.

white, 614. We have several times referred in these descriptions to padded borders for centre-pieces.

An example of one is seen in Fig. 50. The foundation material between the stamped lines is first darned with raw silk, to raise the surface, and is afterwards worked over in button-hole stitch with white Persian Floss. It adds to the beauty of this border to work a row of very short outline stitches in pale green close inside the scallops and the crossbar. The three dots above—which are padded like the border—represent jewels; the middle one is an amethyst, being worked with purple, while the other two are emeralds, which are worked with green. This border is a fitting frame for a design of purple orchids, or for any floral piece showing purple blossoms.

Lest any of our readers should be in doubt about "raw silk," we will add that this is only one name which has been applied to a soft fluffy silk composed of several strands and sold in skeins under the name of Florence Natural Silk. It is made only in shades of white. It is much superior to cotton for padding any kind of raised embroidery, as when the work is a little worn if padded with cotton this may show through and look badly, while if padded with silk the wear will not show.

PRACTICAL PATTERNS FOR EMBROIDERY,—FLORAL, FRUIT AND CONVENTIONAL PIECES.

(Figs. 51, 52, 53, 54, 55, 56, 57, 58, 59, 60, 61, 62 and 63.)

In all the descriptions which follow, the material used for embroidery is Corticelli Fast Dye Wash Silk. The numbers are taken from the Corticelli color card. It takes about six skeins of Roman or Persian Floss for the border of the largest design spoken of here. Smaller pieces take less silk for the same purpose. In many cases the work within the border will require only a single skein or spool of each color in Filo Silk, but this depends on the pattern.

Fig. 51.—Tea Rose Design.

Tea Rose Design (Fig. 51). *Material.*—Persian Floss, white, 614; Filo Silk, white, 614; yellow, 501, 502, 503, 504 and 505; green, 661, 663, 665; bronze, 757; brown, 527; pink, 635.5, 636. *Border.*—

FLORENCE HOME NEEDLE-WORK.

Work scrolls with white Persian Floss in solid button-hole stitch; do all edges of flowers with white Filo Silk, in long and short button-hole stitch, tinting inside of petals with shades of pink, dotting centres with yellow French knots and a touch of pale green. *Flower.*— Work solid in five shades of yellow; use the lightest on the edge of the petals, shading to darker at the base; pad the turn-over petals with cotton or raw silk and work them in the lightest color. *Buds and Leaves.*

FIG. 52.—ROSE DESIGN.

—Work the buds solid with darkest shade in the centre of opening and a lighter one on each side; work the calyx with light green on the tips and dark on the base; do the stems and leaves in the same way, using darker shades for large leaves than for small ones; touches of brown are effective on heavy leaves and stems. This design can be obtained stamped on twenty-two and eighteen inch squares of linen.

FIG. 53.—ROSE BUD DESIGN.

Rose Design (Fig. 52). *Material.* — Persian Floss, white, 615; Filo Silk, white, 615; pink, 572.5, 573.5; green, 064, 782, 783, 784, 785; bronze, 757; brown, 646; red, 655.7, 655.9, 656, 658, 660, 544. *Border.* — Work scrolls with white Persian Floss in solid button-hole stitch, padding slightly; do the edges of small flowers with white Filo Silk in long and short button-hole stitch, tinting inside of the petals with shades of pink, dotting centres with yellow French knots and a touch of golden-brown; back of each group of small flowers and outside the scrolls, there appears a small blank space; fill this with fine darning stitches, done with first shade of green. *Flowers and Buds.* — Work solid in six shades of red (including pink). The lightest color is used on the edge and for the turn-over petals, which are raised high by padding, shading gradually to the darkest red at the base; work bud

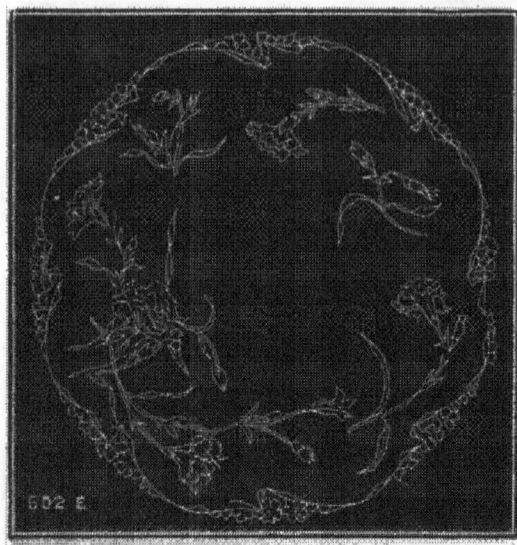

Fig. 54. — Carnation Pink Design.

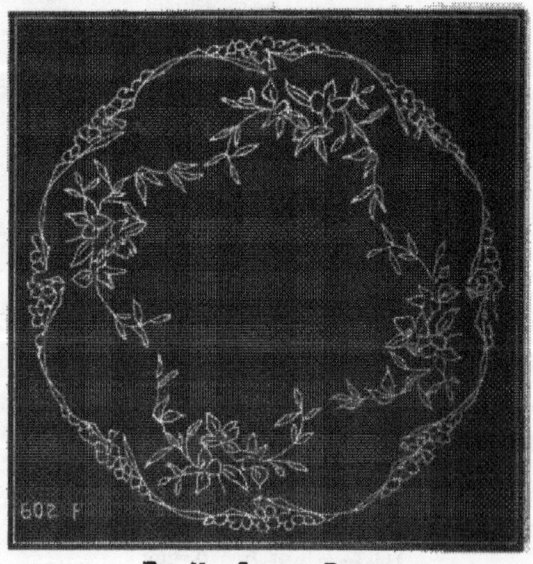

Fig. 55. — Syringa Design.

solid, using dark red in the centre, with lighter on each side; do the calyx with shades of green, lightest on tip and darkest at base.

Stem and Leaf.— Work with shades of green, dark at base and light on point; the veins are dark, and touches of bronze and golden-brown on stems and large leaves improve the effect. This design can be obtained stamped on twenty-two and eighteen inch squares of linen.

ROSE BUD DESIGN (Fig. 53).

Material.—Persian Floss, white, 615; Filo Silk, white, 615; red, 656, 658, 660, 544; green, 781, 782, 783; bronze, 757; yellow, 741, 742; golden-brown, 646.

FIG. 56.—CLOVER DESIGN.

Border.—Work scrolls with white Persian Floss in solid button-hole stitch; do the small flowers in long and short button-hole stitch with white Filo Silk, tinting the petals with two shades of yellow and dotting the centres with golden-brown and a touch of green; fill the spaces

FIG. 57.—CHERRY DESIGN.

back of these flowers and outside the scroll with fine darning stitches in bronze, 757. *Rose Buds.* — Work solid in shades of red Filo Silk, using the darkest for the back petals; work those petals light which appear on top; the lightest shade is to be used on points, shading darker towards base; the calyx is light on points and dark at base, running still darker on the bulb. *Leaves.* — Work solid in shades of green, using lightest on points, shading darker towards centre; do veins and stems in darkest green and bronze-green. This design can be obtained stamped on twenty-two and eighteen inch squares of linen.

CARNATION PINK DESIGN (Fig. 54). *Material.* — Persian Floss, white, 615; Filo Silk, pink, 572, 573, 573.5, 574, 578; green, 662, 663, 664, 666, 757; white, 614; maize, 644.6, 644.7, 644.8, 644.9. *Border.* — Work scrolls with white Persian Floss in solid button-hole stitch, slightly padded with raw silk; do the edges of small flowers with white Filo Silk in long and short button-hole stitch, tinting the insides of petals with shades of light maize and dotting the centres with the darkest shade and a slight touch of green. *Flowers.* — Work the carnations solid in shades of pink; the edges of petals are light, and dark shades are used in centres; the buds show but little pink, and that on the points, where two shades will be enough. *Leaves.* — Work in shades of green, using light on points and dark at the base. This design can be obtained stamped on twenty-two and eighteen inch squares of linen.

FIG. 53. — STRAWBERRY DESIGN.

SYRINGA DESIGN (Fig. 55). *Material.* — Persian Floss, white, 614; Filo Silk, white, 616; green, 661, 662, 663; yellow, 506, 782, 783, 784. *Border.* — Work scrolls with white Persian Floss in solid button-hole stitch, padded slightly; do the edges of small flowers with Filo Silk in long and short button-hole stitch, tinting the insides of petals with shades of green and dotting centres with yellow French knots. *Flower.* — Work solid with white (616) Filo Silk, shading with pale green; the stamens are white and the anthers yellow. *Leaves and Stems.* — Work solid in shades of green (782, 783, 784), using lightest on leaf points, shading darker towards centre and base; do stems in darkest green. This design can be obtained stamped on twenty-two and eighteen inch squares of linen.

CLOVER DESIGN (Fig. 56). *Material.* — Persian Floss, white, 614; Filo Silk, pink, 678, 679, 681; green, 692.9, 693, 694, 695. *Border.* — Work scallops with white Persian Floss in indented button-hole stitch. *Flowers.* — Work solid with Filo Silk in shades of pink. *Leaves and Stems.* — Work with Filo Silk in shades of green, using long and short stitch; do the interlaced stems with the two darkest shades of green in outline.

FIG. 59. — DELFT DESIGN.

This design measures about ten and one-half inches each way and can be obtained stamped on twelve inch squares of linen. It is very attractive when well worked and is an excellent size for many places where a small centre-piece is wanted in this shape.

CHERRY DESIGN (Fig. 57). *Material.* — EE Embroidery Silk, white, 614; Filo Silk, red, 538, 539, 540, 542; green, 832, 581, 582, 583, 584. *Border.* — Work outer edges of scallops with white EE Embroidery Silk in solid button-hole stitch; work the trefoil shape which separates the scallops with Filo Silk in first shade of green, using long and short stitch. *Fruit.* — Work solid in shades of red, piling silk high. *Leaves.* — Work solid in shades of green, using lightest on points; the veins are dark as well as the stems. This design can be obtained stamped on twenty-two, eighteen, twelve and nine inch squares of linen.

STRAWBERRY DESIGN (Fig. 58). *Material.* — Roman Floss, white, 614; Filo Silk, red, 534, 535, 536, 537, 539, 540; green, 581, 781, 782, 783.5, 785; bronze, 752.9. *Border.* — Work scallops in outer edge with Roman Floss in solid button-hole stitch; work the trefoil shape which separates the scallops with Filo Silk in third shade of green, using long and short stitch. *Fruit.* — Work solid and high with shades of red; the seeds which appear on the surface should be done with first shade of green; do the unripe berry in bronze. *Leaves and Stems.* — Work with shades of green, using lightest on the points and small leaves; the veins and stems are dark. This design can be obtained stamped on twenty-two, eighteen, twelve and nine inch squares of linen.

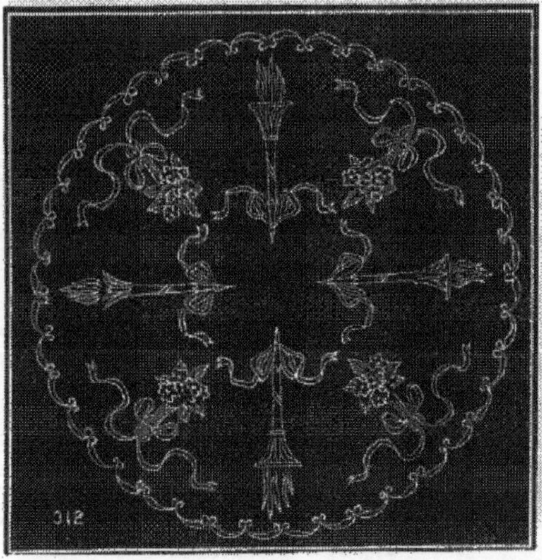

DELFT DESIGN (Fig. 59). *Material.* — Persian Floss, blue, 786; Filo Silk, blue, 789, 791, 792, 793. *Border.* — Work the scallops in button-hole stitch with Persian Floss in blue. *Medallion.* — Work the water lines with Filo Silk, using palest blue, the background in the second shade, and the hull and masts in the darkest shade; work the disc in outline stitch with darkest blue, and the turn-over part in long and short stitch with lighter shade. *Flowers.* — Work with Filo Silk in long and short stitch; use the third shade for the back petals and the next two shades lighter for the front petals; work the small buds in the two darkest shades. *Leaves.* — Work these with Filo Silk in long and short stitch with two lightest shades of blue; use the darkest shade for stems and veins. This design can be obtained stamped on twenty-two, eighteen, twelve and nine inch squares of linen.

EMPIRE DESIGN (Fig. 60). *Material.* — Persian Floss, white, 614; Filo Silk, green, 752.9, 753, 754, 755, 757; purple, 726, 727, 728, 729; pink, 636, 638; flame, 799, 800, 801, 802; maize, 644.7, 644.8, 645,

FIG. 60. — EMPIRE DESIGN.

647. *Border*. — Work the scallops with Persian Floss in white with button-hole stitch. *Bow Knot under Flower*. — Work ribbon solid or in slanting stitch with Filo Silk in lightest pink, using darker shade to outline edges. *Bow Knot under Torch*. — Work solid with Filo Silk in lightest purple, outlining edges with second shade darker. *Violets and Leaves*.—Work with Filo Silk in shades of purple, some blossoms in two light shades, and some in two dark shades; do centre of each flower with lightest maize; do leaves with shades of green, using light at tips and dark toward base; work stems and veins with darkest green. This design can be obtained stamped on twenty-two, eighteen, twelve and nine inch squares of linen.

Fig. 61.—Leaf Design.

Leaf Design (Fig. 61). *Material*.—Persian Floss, green, 782; white, 614; Filo

Fig. 62.—Wild Flower Design.

points with white Persian Floss in solid button-hole stitch; work inner points in the same stitch with green; do cross-bars between with dark green Persian Floss and cat-stitch the spaces between with white Filo Silk; work the eight leaves with two shades of green Filo Silk, using lightest on the edges and darkest for veins and stems; do the leaves in long and short stitch. This pattern is likely to be a great favorite, as it is very attractive in these soft colors. Many other combinations can be worked; among them are autumn leaf colors, which we do not need to describe; the design is also very effective when done in shades of soft brown with white. We advise our readers to use white for the outside in any combination. This design can be obtained stamped on twenty-two, eighteen and twelve inch squares of linen.

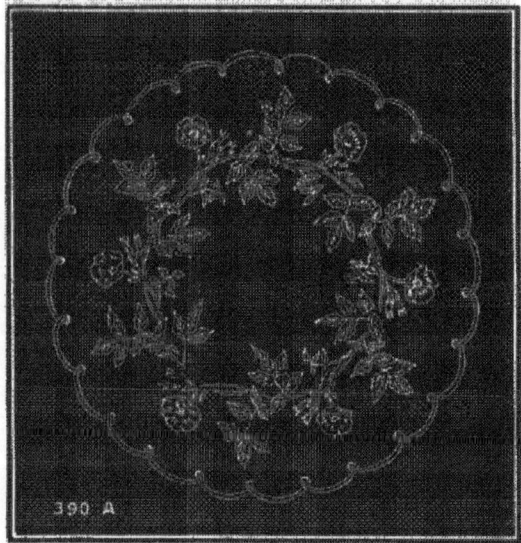

Fig. 63.—Wild Flower Design.

Wild Flower Design (Fig. 62). *Material.*— Persian Floss, yellow, 501; Filo Silk, yellow, 504, 505, 506, 507, 508; green, 781, 782, 783, 784.

Border.— Work scallops with Persian Floss in yellow with button-hole stitch. *Flowers (Wood Sorrel).*— Work solid with Filo Silk in shades of yellow, using dark for back points, lighter for those in front and shading darker to base. *Leaves and Stems.*— Work leaves solid with Filo Silk in shades of green from light to medium, with darker at base; vein them with darkest shade, working stems in same with outline stitch; do braided inner circle with Filo Silk in darkest green. This design can be obtained stamped on twenty-two, eighteen, twelve, nine, seven and six inch linen squares.

Wild Flower Design (Fig. 63). *Material.*— Embroidery Silk, size EE, white, 614; Filo Silk, pink, 636, 637, 638; green, 781, 782, 783, 784, 785; yellow, 505. Use white for border, pink and yellow

Correct Colors for Embroidery

IN

Floral, Fruit and Conventional Designs.

FLOWERS.

The numbers under this head are taken from the Corticelli color card (Fig. 1) and refer to shades used for the blossoms. They do not include the shades required for stems, leaves and tendrils, which are nearly always green. Of this color there are eight distinct groups on the card, which are indicated by the letters a, b, c, d, e, f, g and h, to avoid needless repetition. One of these letters appears as a reference mark against each of the flowers in our list, and shows the group from which shades of green are to be selected for leaves. Under the head of leaves these reference marks are further explained.

Abutilon. — Yellow, Nos. 506 and 507; Red, Nos. 540 and 543; Old Purple, Nos. 673, 674 and 676; and Olive, No. 757 (a).
Apple Blossom. — Pink, Nos. 572, 572.5, 573 and 573.5, and White, No. 615 for petals; and Yellow, No. 506 for centre (b).
Azalea. — Pink, Nos. 572.5, 573, 573.5, 574 and 578; and Red, No. 544 (d).
Azalea. — White, No. 614, slightly tinted with pale Olive Green, No. 781 (d).
Bachelor's-button. — Old Blue, Nos. 821, 822, 823, 824 and 825; or Nos. 744, 745, 746 and 747 (a).
Begonia. — Variegated, Pink, Nos. 636, 637, 638 and 639; Yellow, Nos. 506 and 510; and White, No. 615 (c).
Bitter-sweet. — Red, Nos. 814, 816, 818 and 820 (b).
Buttercup. — Yellow, Nos. 503, 504, 505, 506 and 507 (a).
Cactus. — Red, Nos. 536, 536.5, 537, 538 and 539 (b).
Cactus. — Yellow, Nos. 740, 741, 742, 743 and 743.5 (b).
Cat's-tail. — Brown, Nos. 525.9, 526 and 527 (a).
Chrysanthemum. — Yellow, Nos. 740, 741, 742, 743 and 743.5 (c).
Chrysanthemum. — Old Rose, Nos. 715, 716, 717, 718 and 719 (c).
Chrysanthemum. — Pink, Nos. 636, 637, 638, 639 and 640 (c).
Clematis. — Pink, Nos. 573, 574 and 574.5 (c).
Clematis. — Purple, Nos. 511, 511.5, 512 and 513; Olive, Nos. 780 and 782; and Brown, No. 529 (c).
Clover. — Old Pink, Nos. 678, 679, 680 and 681 (d).
Corn-flower. — Old Blue, Nos. 786, 787, 788, 789 and 791 (a).
Coxcomb. — Red, Nos. 657, 658, 659 and 660 (d).

Crocus. — Yellow, Nos. 742, 743 and 743.5 (c).
Crocus. — White, No. 614; and Yellow, No. 508 (c).
Crocus. — Red-Purple, Nos. 650, 651, 652 and 653; and Yellow No. 743.6 (c).
Cypress. — Pink, Nos. 534, 535, 536 and 536.5 (c).
Daffodil. — Yellow, Nos. 501, 502, 503, 504, 506 and 507 (b).
Daisy. — White, No. 615 for petals; and Yellow, No. 506 for centre (h).
Daisy. — Yellow, Nos. 509 and 510 for petals; and Brown, No. 527 for centre (h).
Fleur-de-lis. — Blue-Purple, Nos. 511, 511.5, 512, 513 and 514; and Yellow, Nos. 506, 507 and 508 (d).
Forget-me-not. — Blue, Nos. 518, 519 and 520 for petals; and Yellow, No. 507 for centre (c).
Geranium. — Pink, Nos. 534, 535, 536, 536.5 and 537 (b).
Geranium. — Red, Nos. 763, 764, 765, 766, 767, 768 and 769 (b).
Gloxinia. — Purple, Nos. 649.9, 650, 651, 652 and 653; and White, No. 614 (c).
Golden-rod. — Yellow, Nos. 503, 504, 505, 506, 507 and 508 (c).
Harebell. — Blue, Nos. 744, 745 and 746 (c).
Heliotrope. — Purple, Nos. 844, 845 and 846; or Nos. 649.9, 650 and 651 (b).
Hibiscus. — Yellow, Nos. 501, 502, 503 and 504 (a).
Hibiscus. — Variety, Cameronii, Yellow, Nos. 740, 741 and 742; and Crimson, Nos. 655.8, 655.9, 657, 658 and 660 (a).
Hibiscus. — Variety, Syrian, Variegated, White, No. 614; Old Pink, No. 679; Yellow, No. 741; and Red, Nos. 540 and 544 (a).
Honeysuckle. — Pink, Nos. 534, 535, 536, 536.5 and 537 (e).
Honeysuckle. — Yellow, Nos. 740, 741, 742, 743 and 743.5; and White, No. 615 (e).
Honeysuckle. — Red, Nos. 655.7, 655.8, 655.9, 656, 657 and 658 (e).
Hyacinth. — Pink, Nos. 636, 637, 638, 639 and 640 (c).
Hyacinth. — Purple, Nos. 726, 727, 728, 729 and 729.5 (c).
Iris. — Red-Purple, Nos. 649.9, 650, 651, 652 and 653; Yellow, Nos. 742, 743 and 743.5; and White, No. 614 (d).
Jasmine. — White, No. 615 (a).
Jasmine. — Yellow, Nos. 502, 503, 504 and 505 (a).
Jonquil. — Yellow, Nos. 503, 504, 505 and 506 (b).
Lilac. — Red-Purple, Nos. 649.9, 650, 651 and 652 (d).
Lily of the Valley. — White, No. 615, slightly tinted with Olive Green, No. 780 (c).
Lily. — Variety, Calla, White, No. 616; and Yellow, No. 743.5 (c).
Lily. — Variety, Easter, White, No. 614; Olive, No. 782; and Yellow, No. 506 (c).
Magnolia. — White, No. 615; Green, No. 663; and Yellow, No. 506 (h).

FLORENCE HOME NEEDLE-WORK. 73

Mignonette. — Olive Green, No. 781; Copper, No. 771; and Red, No. 768 (c).

Morning-glory. — Pink, Nos. 636, 637, 638 and 639 (a).

Narcissus. — White, No. 615; and Yellow, Nos. 503 and 510 (b).

Nasturtium. — Yellow, Nos. 741, 743, 743.5, 743.6, 743.7, 743.8 and 743.9; or darker line, Nos. 810, 811, 812, 813, 814, 815, 816, 817, 818, 819 and 820 (c).

Orchid. — White, No. 615; Red, No. 542; Purple, No. 652; and Orange, No. 508 (e).

Orchid. — Variety, Miltonia Spectabilis, Purple, Nos. 726, 727, 728, 729 and 729.5; Yellow, Nos. 740, 741, 504 and 505; and Red, Nos. 660 and 544 (a).

Orchid. — Variety, Saccolabium Ampullaceum, Old Pink, Nos. 679, 680, 681 and 682; and Yellow, No. 504 (a).

Orchid. — Variety, Beautiful Dendrobium, White, No. 616; Olive, Nos. 661, 663, 752.9 and 753; and Yellow, Nos. 506 and 508 (a).

Pansy. — Yellow, Nos. 743 and 743.6; and Purple, Nos. 726, 728 and 729.5 (c).

Pansy. — Yellow, Nos. 505, 506, 507 and 508; and Blue-Purple, Nos. 511.5, 512 and 513; or Purple, Nos. 844, 846 and 848 (c).

Pansy. — Red-Purple, Nos. 650, 651 and 652; and Yellow, Nos. 742, 743 and 743.5 (c).

Pink. — Variety, Carnation, Pink, Nos. 572.5, 573, 573.5, 574 and 575 (d).

Pink. — Variety, Carnation, Pink, Nos. 535, 536, 536.5, 537 and 538; or Nos. 636, 637, 638 and 639 (d).

Pink. — Variety, Carnation, Yellow, Nos. 501, 502 and 503; and Cream White, No. 616 (d).

Pink. — Variety, Carnation, White, No. 615 or No. 616 (d).

Poppy. — Variety, California, Yellow, Nos. 504, 505, 506, 507 and 508 (b).

Poppy. — Red, Nos. 538, 539, 541, 542 and 543 (d).

Primrose. — Variety, English, Yellow, Nos. 503, 504 and 505 (c).

Rhododendron. — Pink, Nos. 572, 572.5, 573, 573.5 and 574 (a).

Rose. — Variety, Wild, Pink, Nos. 572, 572.5 and 573; and Yellow, No. 506; or Pink, Nos. 573, 573.5, 574 and 575; and Yellow, No. 507 (c).

Rose. — Yellow, Nos. 501, 502, 503, 504 and 505 (c).

Rose. — Variety, Jacqueminot, Red, Nos. 658, 659 and 660 for petals; and Yellow, No. 506 for centre (c).

Sweet-pea. — Old Pink, Nos. 678, 679 and 680; Dull Purple, Nos. 674 and 675; and White, No. 614 (c).

Sweet-pea. — Pink, Nos. 636, 637, 638, 639 and 640; or Nos. 678, 679, 680 and 681; or Nos. 572, 572.5, 573 and 573.5; and White, No. 614 (c).

Sweet-pea. — White, Nos. 615 and 616, slightly tinted with pale Olive Green, No. 780 (c).

Thistle. — Purple, Nos. 649.9, 650, 651 and 652 (*b*).
Trailing Arbutus. — Pink, Nos. 572, 572.5, 573, 573.5 and 574 (*c*).
Trumpet-flower. — Red, Nos. 538, 539 and 540; and Yellow, Nos. 507, 508 and 509 (*c*).
Tulip. — Yellow, Nos. 501, 502, 503, 504 and 505 (*d*).
Tulip. — Old Pink, Nos. 678, 679 and 680; and White, No. 614 (*d*). The shades of pink are subordinate to the white, and when properly distributed in the flower it is a beautiful subject for embroidery.
Tulip. — Scarlet, Nos. 538, 539, 540 and 542 (*d*).
Verbena. — Pink, Nos. 573.5 and 574.5; and White, No. 616 (*d*).
Violet. — Variety, English, Purple, Nos. 649.9, 650, 651 and 65., or Nos. 725, 726, 727, 728 and 729 (*a*).
Water-lily. — White, No. 615 for petals; and Yellow, No. 506 for centre (*e*).
Wild Flowers. — Most of these which are suitable for embroidery have been already included in the foregoing list, and no special colors are required for others; the chief characteristic of the uncultivated blossoms is paler coloring, owing to the fact that they bloom in shady places.
Wistaria. — Purple, Nos. 843, 844, 845, 846, 847 and 848 (*c*).

LEAVES.

The numbers under this head are taken from the Corticelli color card (Fig. 1), on which can be found eight different lines of green shades.

For convenience each of these groups has been given a designating letter, which is printed in *italic*. One of these reference marks is appended to the description of each flower, as seen on the preceding pages, and indicates the particular group which is suitable for the leaves.

The color numbers are given below for each of the eight groups, but it is not expected that every number in a group will be used for any one piece of embroidery. Three shades are often enough, and not more than six are needed for a very close shading. The dark shades are used the least.

Group a. — Olive Green, Nos. 580.5, 581, 581.5, 582, 583, 583.5, 584, 585 and 586.
Group b. — Olive Green, Nos. 692.8, 692.9, 693, 694, 694.5, 695, 695.5 and 696.
Group c. — Olive Green, Nos. 780, 781, 782, 783, 783.5, 784 and 785.
Group d. — Olive Green, Nos. 661, 662, 663, 664, 665 and 666.
Group e. — Olive Green, Nos. 752.9, 753, 754, 755 and 757. This

For a line of olive-green shades adapted to the leaves of flowers in general, Group *a* is good.

Special selections from other green lines may be made to suit the taste, more depending upon harmonious relation to the colors used for the flower than the natural color of the leaf. All the numbers given for leaves are shades of green.

FRUIT, Etc.

The numbers are taken from color card (Fig. 1).

Acorn. — Brown, Nos. 620, 621 and 622 (*a*).

Cherry. — Red, Nos. 538, 539, 540 and 542 (*a*).

Currant. — Red, Nos. 538, 539 and 540; and Black, No. 612 (*a*).

Delft Designs. — Conventional patterns, introducing medallions enclosing Dutch landscape and sea views, with windmills, boats and other objects, are called Delft. The embroidery is done in shades of blue peculiar to the china made in Holland. The Delft Blue shades are 786, 787, 788, 789, 791, 792, 793, 794, 795 and 796, ten shades, ranging from extreme light to dark. Blue crockery is often seen which resembles that made in Holland, but which is the product of other countries. The shades which match this are Nos. 821, 822, 823, 824 and 825.

Dresden Figures. — Minute representations of some of our common flowers, in detached sprays, buds and leaves scattered over the surface of white linen, are spoken of as Dresden figures.

Rose buds, pinks, buttercups and the batchelor's-button are popular subjects.

The figures being very small, will not require many shades of one color. Pink, Nos. 637, 638, 639 and 640, or Nos. 572.5, 573, 573.5 and 574, are good shades for this work. Old Blue, Nos. 788, 789 and 791; or Nos. 736.5, 737 and 738 are useful; Blue, Nos. 519, 520 and 521; Purple, Nos. 727, 728 and 729; Yellow, Nos. 741, 742, 743 and 743 5; and Old Pink, Nos. 679, 680 and 681, are also good. Use Group *e* or Group *c* for shades of green.

Those persons who are fortunate enough to possess some rare pieces of Dresden china will find much pleasure in embroidery of this style, using silk in the colors which appear on the china.

Empire and Colonial Designs. — Wreaths, festoons, garlands and the flaming torch are the principal conventional ornaments. The special colors used are Empire Green, Nos. 803, 804, 805, 806, 807 and 808; Old Blue, Nos. 736.5, 737 and 738; and Flame, Nos. 797, 798, 799, 800, 801 and 802.

Gooseberry. — Variety called White, Olive, Nos. 752 9 and 753; and Black, No. 612 (*a*).

Grape. — Old Purple, Nos. 672, 673, 674, 675 and 676 (*a*).

Holly. — Red. Nos. 539 and 541 (*a*).

Jewelled Designs. — Conventional patterns, introducing scrolls, festoons and other styles of ornament, studded with shapes in imitation of jewels. These shapes are stamped on linen and worked in raised embroidery with Corticelli Filo Silk in the colors of the precious stones. These vary in shade, so, in some cases, more than one number is given.
Amethyst — Purple, Nos. 649.9, 650 and 651; *Emerald* — Green, Nos. 548.5, 549, 550 and 551; *Garnet* — Red, Nos. 541 and 542; *Pearl* — White, No. 614; *Ruby* — Red, Nos. 655.9, 656, 657, 658 and 659; *Sapphire* — Blue, No. 749; *Topaz* — Yellow, Nos. 644.8, 644.9 and 645; *Turquoise* — Blue, No. 623.
Some other pale tints in green, blue and yellow are employed in this jewel work, such as Nos. 780, 781, 752.9, 661, 692.9, 699, 519, 750, 501, 803 and 831.

Mistletoe. — White, No. 615; and Brown, No. 622 (*c*).

Pine Cone. — Tan-Brown, Nos. 620, 621 and 622 (*b*).

Pomegranate. — Copper, Nos. 771, 773 and 774; and Red, Nos. 719, 720 and 722 (*a*).

Strawberry. — Red, Nos. 534, 535, 536, 537, 539 and 540. The seeds which appear on the surface of the berry are represented by using light Olive Green, No. 581. The unripe berry is worked with shade No. 752.9, and the stem and hull with shades Nos. 782, 784 and 785 (*c*).

Sunshine Effects. — Nile Green, No. 699, Pink, No. 573, Yellow, No. 506, Lavender, No. 650, Yellow, No. 741, and White, No. 614, properly combined, will produce the effect of sunshine, as in the rainbow and other phases of nature.

SEA-WEED COLORS.

The bottom of the sea having been drawn upon by artists for decorative work in embroidery, a few words on the peculiar colors which mark the vegetation of the ocean as it appears growing, or when first cast by storms upon the land, may be useful to those who see the designs, but who are remote from the seashore, and cannot themselves look at the so-called sea weed or grasses.

The predominant colors are red, green and brown; the following lines selected from the Corticelli color card will be useful in embroidery of this kind, viz. : —

Give All the Particulars.

IF YOU WISH TO ORDER some of our Fast Dye Silk for your embroidery, tell your dealer explicitly what you require. It is not enough to say Wash Silk — that is a broad term and applies to several sizes and kinds; you should therefore include in your requisition these details: —
1. The brand — Corticelli.
2. The variety — stating whether Roman Floss, Persian Floss, Rope, Etching, Lace or Filo Silk is wanted.
3. The size — not all of the Corticelli Silk is thus designated, but in those cases where the size appears on the label it is well to mention it, as it has a definite meaning.
4. The color — number as selected from our color card.
5. Mention the form in which you want the silk. Filo Silk and the EE Embroidery Silk can be had on spools or in skeins; the other kinds come in skeins only. Consult the advertising pages of this book, where engravings of each variety can be seen.

NONOTUCK SILK CO.,
FLORENCE, MASS.

Dealers and Art Needlework Teachers

Unacquainted with the superior quality and finish of

Corticelli Wash Silk

Are invited to write us for full information regarding our constantly increasing line of Art Embroidery Silks and Flosses. We appreciate all inquiries.

Nonotuck Silk Company,
Florence, Mass.

Florence Silk Mosaic.

A beautiful material for the four-in-hand scarf, admitting of easy hand embroidery; colors — cream-white, black, navy-blue and wood-brown.

The stitches used in Mosaic Embroidery are fully illustrated in "Florence Home Needlework" for 1895. Patterns of this Mosaic — enough for a four-in-hand scarf, — five spools of silk, a suitable needle, with designs and directions complete, will be mailed to any address on receipt of eighty cents.

Nonotuck Silk Co.,
Florence, Mass.

Florence Silk Gloves for Gentlemen.

These goods are lined throughout with soft silk. They are made without seams either inside or out, consequently cannot rip. Being full-fashioned, they fit the hand perfectly, and are in all respects the warmest, least cumbersome, and most genteel and durable glove for winter wear now in the market. Sizes, Nos. 1, 2 and 3; large, medium and small. If you cannot get a pair from your dealer, we will mail them to you on receipt of $2.00. Their color is black.

Nonotuck Silk Co.,
Florence, Mass.

Florence Natural Silk.
(Raw Silk.)

This is a soft silk which is now used for padding the surfaces of designs in raised embroidery, a style which is now popular. Jewels, padded borders done in button-hole stitch, rose petals and other kinds of high work require it for the best results. It is made only in shades of white, is sold in skeins and will wash well.

Nonotuck Silk Co.,
Florence, Mass.

Florence Silk Underwear

FOR GENTLEMEN AND LADIES.

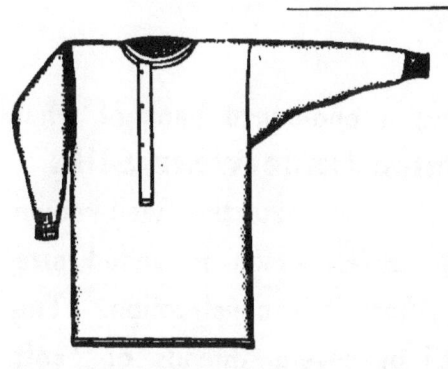

Highest Award at "World's Columbian Exposition," Chicago, 1893.

FULL FASHIONED.

The attention of those persons who wish to promote health and comfort is invited to the advantages this underwear has over that made from other materials.

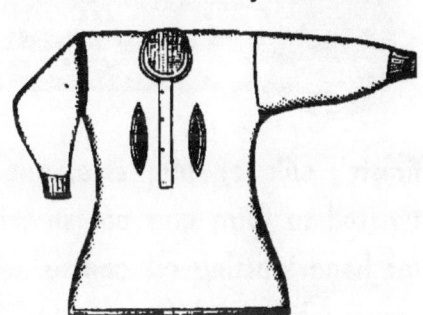

Manufactured from strictly pure, "soft finish" silk, which is entirely free from any dye-stuff or other foreign substance which might cause irritation, without seams, and trimmed in a superior manner, a degree of comfort and protection from cold is obtained in its use not to be had in garments of any other material.

PRICE LIST MAILED ON APPLICATION.

Nonotuck Silk Co., Sole Manufacturers,
FLORENCE, MASS.

Florence Underwear Silk.

SOFT FINISH.

THE engraving shows a one-ounce hank of what is called **Florence Underwear Silk.**

It is considerably coarser than the well-known **Florence Knitting Silk,** which is called size No. 300, and it differs from it in construction. The hank silk is composed of several threads of "soft

finish" silk of fine size, put together and slightly twisted to form one coarse thread specially intended for hand knitting on coarse needles. The colors are cream white and flesh color, and will bear washing without injury. Ask your storekeeper for these goods. If he cannot furnish you, write to the makers, who will have the silk mailed to any address in the United States at the rate of sixty cents per ounce, postage paid.

NONOTUCK SILK CO.,

FLORENCE, MASS.

YOU NEED THIS SILK.

If you are intending to do any "Lace Embroidery" or "Honiton work" you need a supply of the silk

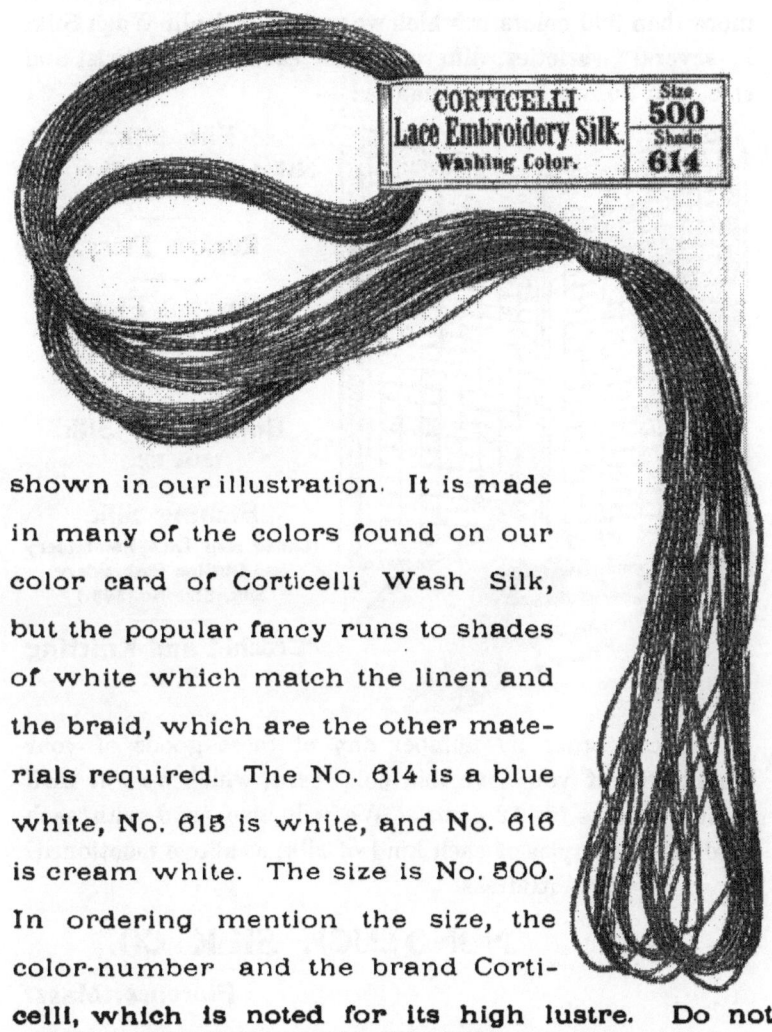

shown in our illustration. It is made in many of the colors found on our color card of Corticelli Wash Silk, but the popular fancy runs to shades of white which match the linen and the braid, which are the other materials required. The No. 614 is a blue white, No. 615 is white, and No. 616 is cream white. The size is No. 500. In ordering mention the size, the color-number and the brand Corticelli, which is noted for its high lustre. Do not allow substitutes to be imposed upon you.

NONOTUCK SILK CO., Florence, Mass.

Corticelli Color Card.

WASHING COLORS.

Short pieces of silk are attached to this card, showing more than 300 colors in which we make Corticelli Wash Silk, in several* varieties, differing from each other in twist and size, and known by these names: —

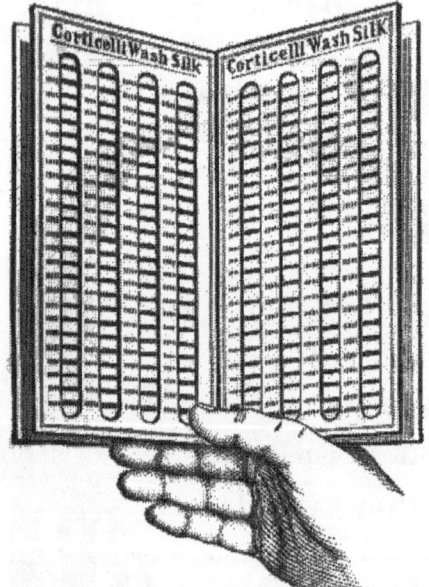

Filo Silk.
(Called also Filo Floss and Filo Selle.)

Roman Floss.

***Persian Floss.**

Rope Silk.

Embroidery Silk.
(Size EE.)

Etching Silk.
(Called also Lace Embroidery and Outline Embroidery Silk, Size No. 500.)

***Crochet and Knitting Silk.**

You can order by number any of these goods of your storekeeper if you have this color card, which we will mail to any address for 12 cents. We will also send with each card small samples of each kind of silk, as above mentioned. Address

NONOTUCK SILK CO.,

Florence, Mass.

---

* The line of colors in the Crochet and Knitting Silk, also the Persian Floss, is not so extensive, but each color in which this kind of silk is sold is indicated.

CORTICELLI

FAST DYE
WASH SILK.

Smooth Working, High Luster.

Dyed by our own original method.

For Decorative Art Needlework
IT CANNOT BE EXCELLED.

Made in Over Three Hundred Fast Colors.

Made only by the
NONOTUCK SILK COMPANY,
Florence, Mass.

Sold by All Enterprising Merchants.

Corticelli Wash Silk.

UNFADING DYES.

Highest Award, World's Fair, Chicago, 1893. Awarded Gold Medal and Special Diploma of Honor, California International Exposition, 1894.

Under this head buyers have the choice of several distinct varieties of silk thread, differing from each other as to size and twist. They are intended for various kinds of fancy work, on materials heavy, medium and light, which require washing. The line of colors is very extensive, and they are

warranted not to "run" or to injure in any way the most delicate fabric when washed in warm water and "Ivory" soap, or any other good soap.

Of the engravings used to illustrate this subject, those showing silk on spools are actual size, while others, showing silk in skeins, are reduced one-half.

The different varieties are described and illustrated as follows: —

CORTICELLI ROPE SILK.

Washing Colors.

[See engraving on preceding page.]

This is a *very* coarse silk, used for bold designs, either in outline or solid embroidery, on heavy material, and where rapid execution is desired. Each skein bears a ticket on which appears the brand Corticelli, as well as the size and color numbers.

CORTICELLI ROMAN FLOSS.

Washing Colors.

This silk is slack twisted and has a very high lustre. It is finer than Rope Silk but much coarser than Filo Silk.

It is used where the designs are large, and quick work is desired, with good effect. Each skein bears a ticket on which appears the brand Corticelli and the color number.

Corticelli Embroidery Silk.

Size EE -- Washing Colors.

THIS kind of Wash Embroidery Silk is probably more extensively used than any other for general work. It is specially recommended for Mosaic Embroidery, which is a novelty in fancy work of great beauty.

Buyers should select the spools for this work, as they keep the silk clean and prevent shop-wear and fraying. In this way they save time and money, by avoiding waste and inconvenience, and at the same time improve their workmanship.

Observe the labels and note the brand Corticelli and the size (EE) on one end of each spool; on the other end the words "Wash Silk — Fast Color" should appear.

When Corticelli EE Wash Embroidery Silk is sold in skeins it is put up in the twisted form, as seen in the engraving. Each skein and spool bears a ticket on which appears the brand Corticelli, as well as the size (EE) and color number.

CORTICELLI FILO SILK.
Washing Colors.

(Called also Filo Floss and Filo Selle.)

These goods are adapted to a wide range of art needlework. For light and delicate embroidery use the thread singly; for heavier work use two threads in combination.

Filo silk may now be bought on spools, which keep the silk clean and prevent shopwear and fraying. In this way you save time and money, by avoiding waste and inconvenience, at the same time improving your workmanship. The color number appears on every spool.

Corticelli Filo Silk is also extensively sold in skeins; each skein bears a guarantee tag branded Corticelli. Buyers should look for this name on spools and on skeins.

CORTICELLI ETCHING SILK.

SIZE No. 500. WASHING COLORS.

(Called also Outline Embroidery Silk and Lace Embroidery Silk.)

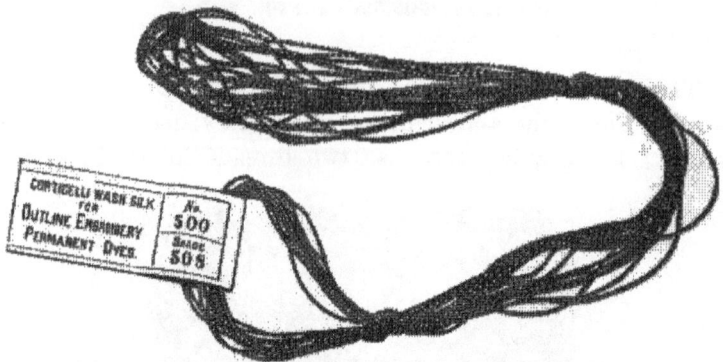

This is a medium size of silk, finer than EE, and suitable for outline work or etching. It is used by the best needle-workers in connection with the slacker twisted kinds, affording a pleasing contrast and producing more artistic work. It is also well adapted to Lace Embroidery or Honiton work. Each skein bears a ticket on which appears the brand Corticelli, as well as the size and color numbers.

CORTICELLI PERSIAN FLOSS.

This is a new variety, lately introduced, which will prove very useful. It is about twice the size of Filo Silk and will be much used for button-hole work on the edges

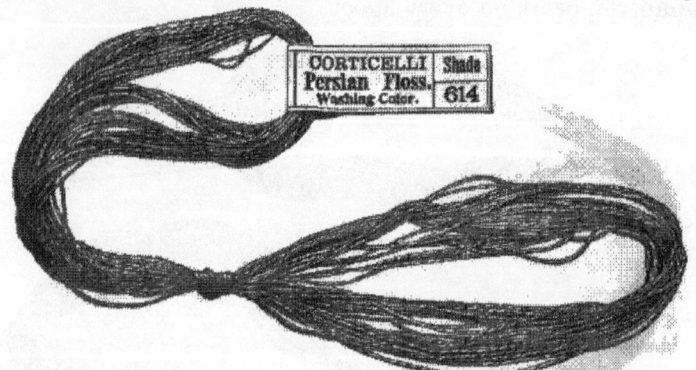

of doilies and centre-pieces, as well as for solid embroidery in some kinds of bold designs where large surfaces are to be covered.

The number of colors in this kind of silk is more limited. It is now furnished in the following lines only, viz.:—

Nos. 501 to 509, yellow.
Nos. 517 to 521, blue.
Nos. 535 to 540, pink to scarlet.
Nos. 572 to 574.5, pink.
Nos. 614 to 616.5, white to cream.

Nos. 636 to 640, old-pink.
Nos. 644.6 to 647, golden brown.
Nos. 649.9 to 658, lilac to purple.
Nos. 780 to 785, olive.
Nos. 786 to 794, Delft blue.

Nos. 803 to 805, Empire green.

These numbers are taken from Corticelli color card.

Corticelli Purse Twist.

FAST DYES -- WASHING COLORS.

The great popularity of this brand of Purse Twist is obtained by the excellence of its colors, the peculiarity of its twist, and the facility with which it may be wrought into those exquisite designs known to women of past generations almost as well as to those of the present time.

There are in existence to-day purses made nearly half a century ago of PURSE SILK, still preserving, in a remarkable degree, their original beauty. A silk purse, well designed and executed from *Corticelli Purse Twist*, makes an elegant and enduring token of friendship. This well-known brand may be obtained of any enterprising merchant.

CAUTION.

Purchasers should notice carefully the black spool with the name CORTICELLI on one end. The genuine is put up only in this way.

CORTICELLI LACE SILK.

Three-cord Crochet.

This is a new silk thread of peculiar construction and great beauty, made expressly for Passementeries, or for crochet work done over rings or moulds of other forms; also for Tatting, Netting, Knitting or any other work where open and fancy patterns in lace effects are desired. Buyers should look for the words "Fast Dye" and "Washing Color" on one end of each spool; on the other end the words "Corticelli Lace Silk, No. 300" will appear. An established reputation of nearly 60 years goes with this brand.

Corticelli Knitting and Crochet Silk.

FAST COLORS.

HIGH LUSTRE.
For Knitting, Crocheting or Embroidery.

Manufactured from the highest grade of selected raw silk. Its size is uniform and the colors are produced by fast dyes of great brilliancy. It is well adapted for knitting fine hosiery, mittens and other articles. It is much used for Crocheted Silk Scarfs, which are done with the crochet needle according to illustrated directions given in "Florence Home Needlework," 1891 and 1892. It is also much used for other kinds of crochet work as well as for embroidery on wash material.

Dealers keep a large variety of colors in size No. 300. No. 500 (fine) is made in shades of white only. Each ball contains one-half ounce of silk, and the weight is warranted full.

Corticelli Crochet Silk.

WHIP-CORD TWIST.

This engraving is a very accurate representation of small balls of Crochet Silk. Each ball contains 25 yards of silk of the three-cord variety. The colors are fast and the silk may be advantageously used for work other than

crochet. Buyers seeking crochet silk in greater lengths will ask for the one-half ounce balls, as illustrated and described above.

Florence Knitting and Crochet Silk.

Soft Finish. Free from Poisonous Dyes. Strictly Pure.

This well-known silk is suitable for knitting mittens, stockings and other articles of wearing apparel which require washing. Any fabric made from it, whether knitted, crocheted or woven, may be washed without the slightest injury to color or texture.

Black, white and colors are sold in these sizes, viz., Nos. 300 and 500, coarse and fine, respectively. Each ball of No. 300 contains one-half ounce of silk, measuring 150 yards. Each ball of No. 500 contains one-half ounce of silk, measuring 250 yards.

FLORENCE DARNING SILK.

Soft Finish. Prepared expressly for Repairs on Silk, Woollen, Lisle Thread or Cotton Stockings and Undergarments.

Stockings darned with this silk last much longer, and are free from the disagreeable bunches caused by the use of wool or cotton yarns for mending purposes.

In buying **new** hosiery, of whatever material, ladies will greatly increase its durability by "running" the heels and toes with **Florence Darning Silk.** This process, by reason of the soft and pliable nature of the silk, does not cause discomfort to the wearer.

Sold by all Enterprising Dealers.

Corticelli Roll Braid.

In making a lady's costume, a good Worsted Braid for the bottom of the skirt is second only in importance to good Sewing Silk and Button-hole Twist, hence every one who knows the guarantee which the brand CORTICELLI gives will be glad to find in the principal stores not only the Silk and Twist, but neat and attractive rolls of Corticelli Worsted Braid to match all the seasonable shades of dress goods.

These braids contain only the best wool, and are made of 61 threads of standard size, in the braiding and coloring of which the same care is taken which has given the brand *Corticelli* an enviable reputation wherever found.

Corticelli Glove Mending Silk.

A silk thread of fine size and peculiar twist is required for repairing gloves neatly by hand. Such a thread in a variety of seasonable colors in a convenient form for immediate use is shown in this engraving. Each braid contains about 300 yards of silk divided into 25 glove shades. A needleful of any one of these colors can quickly be drawn out without disturbing the remaining threads.

These braids can now be found for sale in all the leading notion and dry-goods stores.

Florence Silk Socks,
FOR INFANTS.

Special Award, World's Fair, Chicago, 1893.

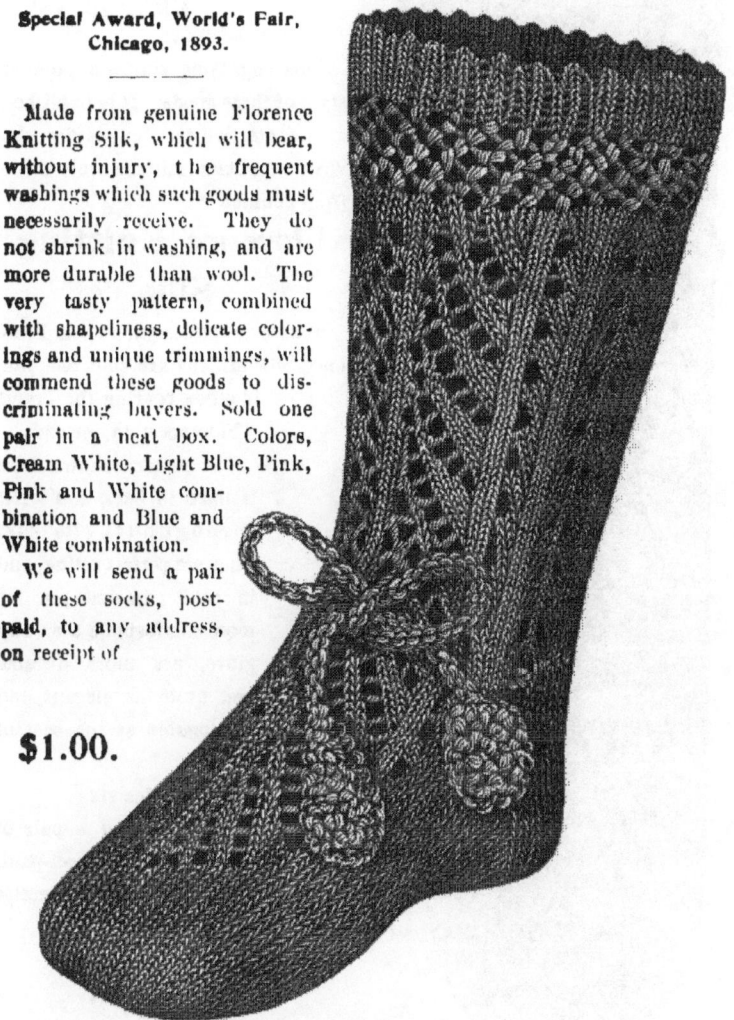

Made from genuine Florence Knitting Silk, which will bear, without injury, the frequent washings which such goods must necessarily receive. They do not shrink in washing, and are more durable than wool. The very tasty pattern, combined with shapeliness, delicate colorings and unique trimmings, will commend these goods to discriminating buyers. Sold one pair in a neat box. Colors, Cream White, Light Blue, Pink, Pink and White combination and Blue and White combination.

We will send a pair of these socks, postpaid, to any address, on receipt of

$1.00.

[The engraving shows nearly the full size.]

Nonotuck Silk Company, Florence, Mass.

Florence Silk Mittens.

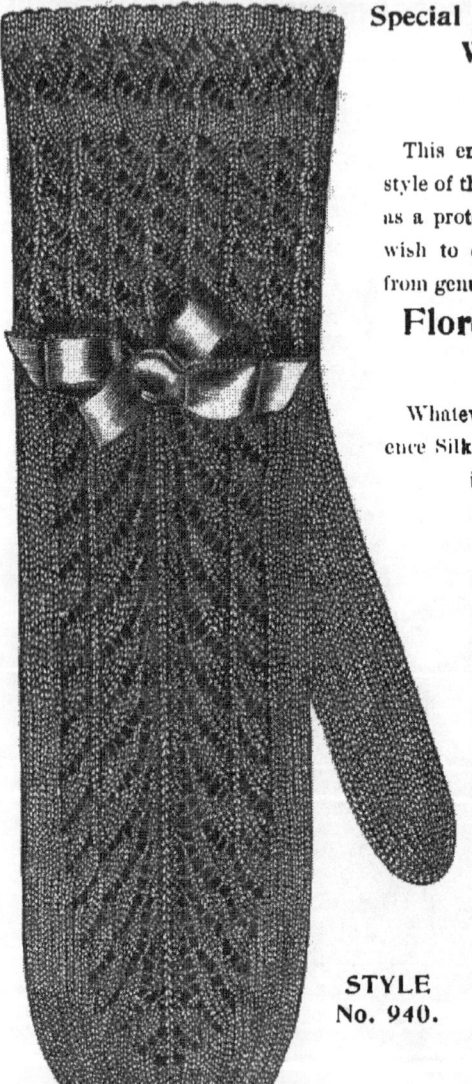

Special Award,
World's Fair,
Chicago, 1893.

This engraving shows a popular style of these goods. It is published as a protection for those ladies who wish to obtain mittens well made from genuine

Florence Knitting Silk.

Whatever the design, all real Florence Silk Mittens are sold one pair in a box bearing the brand "Florence" on one end.

The pattern shown here is lined in back and wrist throughout with silk. They are perfect fitting, and in cold climates are far more comfortable than any glove, are more durable and quite as elegant and fashionable as the best of gloves.

Sold by dealers.

We will send a pair of these mittens, post-paid, to any address, on receipt of

STYLE
No. 940.

$1.50.

[Engraving one-half actual size.]

NONOTUCK SILK COMPANY, Florence, Mass.

Florence Silk Mittens.

FOR CHILDREN.

Special Award, World's Fair, Chicago, 1893.

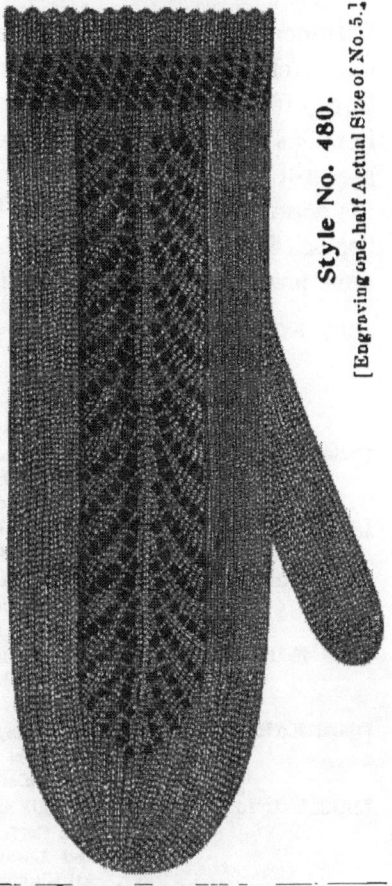

Style No. 480.

[Engraving one-half Actual Size of No. 5.]

This engraving shows style No. 480 of these goods. The wrist and fancy open-work back are lined throughout with silk. They are made of genuine Florence Knitting Silk. Each pair is placed in a fancy box bearing the brand "Florence." Sold by enterprising dealers in these colors and sizes:—
No. 6 and No. 7, Cream White and Light Blue. No. 5 and No. 6, Black, Seal Brown, Garnet and Navy.

Size No. 7 is suitable for children one year or less of age. Size No. 6 is suitable for children from one to three years of age. Size No. 5 is suitable for children from three to five years of age.

For $1.00 we will send, post-paid, to any address, one pair of these mittens of either size.

Nonotuck Silk Co.,
FLORENCE, MASS.

Florence Silk Mittens.
FOR GENTLEMEN.
(Not Illustrated.)

Seamless and lined throughout; superior to gloves, and by many preferred to them. They take up little room in the pocket when not in use, and for walking and driving are superior to mittens made of leather as a protection from cold. We will send, post-paid, to any address, one pair of these mittens for $2.00.

Nonotuck Silk Co., Florence, Mass.

"Florence Home Needle-work" Series

Under this title we have published annually for ten yea[rs] our pamphlet containing comprehensive illustrated descri[p]tions of subjects which come under this head. These pu[b]lications have been in good demand, and the older editio[ns] are still asked for by many who get the later numbers, [as] the contents are very different for each year. The followi[ng] list briefly explains the character of the nine numbers whi[ch] have preceded the present edition.

1887 Edition.—Crochet Silk Bead-work is the leading subject, for wh[ich] three complete and rare Alphabets have been s[pe]cially engraved.
This edition also contains valuable illustrated rules [for] Silk Mittens, Stockings, Laces, etc., etc.

1888 Edition.—Drawn-work, Damask Stitches, Italian, Tapestry, Outl[ine] and Cross-stitch Embroidery, with Crochet, are [the] subjects. All are fully illustrated.

1889 Edition.—Subjects: Tatting, Netting and Embroidery. Replete w[ith] illustrations and clear description.

1890 Edition.—Crochet and Embroidery are leading subjects. The f[irst] chapter gives instructions for a Crocheted Silk Sc[arf] in shell stitch. Each subject is profusely illustrate[d].

1891 Edition.—The subjects are Crocheted Silk Slippers, Scarfs, Be[lts,] Beaded Bags, Macramé Lace, Embroidery, etc., w[ith] 140 engravings.

1892 Edition.—Irish Lace, Sewing, Crocheted Scarfs, Belts, Gart[ers,] Passementeries and other "Fascinating Fancy-w[ork] Fads" are explained by 160 engravings, fully describ[ed].

1893 Edition.—Reeling Raw Silk at the World's Fair is one subject. [The] others are Corticelli Darning, Corticelli Drawn-w[ork,] Crocheted Lamp Shades, Pillow Lace and Embr[oid]ery. All illustrated.

1894 Edition.—Subjects: Corticelli Darning, Knitting, Crochet and "C[or]rect Colors for Flowers." All illustrated.

1895 Edition.—Subjects: Lace Embroidery or Honiton-work, Mosaic [Em]broidery, Scarfs, Necktie, Sofa Pillow, Suspend[ers,] Crochet and "Correct Colors for Flowers." W[ith] many illustrations.

Any one of these books will be mailed on receipt of [six] cents, or all of them for fifty-four cents. Mention year [when] ordering. Each edition contains 96 pages.

Nonotuck Silk Co., Florence, Mass.

www.ingramcontent.com/pod-product-compliance
Lightning Source LLC
Chambersburg PA
CBHW032238080426
42735CB00008B/914